T0157498

BRAIN DEAD BIDEN

POLITICAL SATIRE

GATORMAN

authorHOUSE

AuthorHouse™
1663 Liberty Drive
Bloomington, IN 47403
www.authorhouse.com
Phone: 833-262-8899

Published by AuthorHouse 04/24/2024

ISBN: 979-8-8230-2127-2 (sc)
ISBN: 979-8-8230-2126-5 (e)

Library of Congress Control Number: 2024901765

Print information available on the last page.

This book is printed on acid-free paper.

From the Author, the mega big red Gator

You are about to be exposed to a comical, political satire. All research was obtained from is far left ABC, CBS, NBC, MSNBC, Good Morning Joe, Rachel Maddow joy in the view for all correct information was 98% accurate Fox News station.

the line radical left news outlets in the 95 correct right-wing outlets as listed below corn, pop Biden in his pitiful collection of Marxist, socialist, and communist senate, Congress vice president in a cabinet. This book contains bloopers, blunders, and disasters by our brain Dead Joe. The story is that demonic Democrats do not let your alligator mouth overload your hummingbird asses respectfully to the big mega red gator. Joe, Biden, 2020 radical democrats battle cry, he believed in the Bible his favorite scripture was First Corinthians 14 and 38 is states if any man be ignorant let him be ignorant Joe Biden is ignorant, seven days a week 24 hours a day vote for intelligence, Donald J Trump lead America to infinity and beyond

Information on the Author. I am a 76-year-old 100% disabled Vietnam veteran and a retired government supervisor. I believe the best qualified for any job should be selected not based on political belief. I have said if I went to the White House and saw every Democratic political person lying on the White House lawn screaming their brains were on fire, I would not take out my fire hose and urinate in their ears to put out the fires. Why? brains do not burn, and it is a fact Democrats do not have any brains between their ears.

This political satire, the great insurrection of the USA, by the radical left, Joe Corn-hole fired thousands of essential workers and deprived all the citizens of the USA of essential products and needed resources like gas and oil in a below-zero winter. Welcome to the Inflation Nation, complements of corn hole, pop, drag queen, Biden, King, drag queen lover, Joe Biden.

Again, I am a 76-year-old and a 100% disabled Vietnam veteran. I served three tours in the combat zone from 1966 to 1969 during my second combat tour late one night I and two other fellow veterans were walking back to base when we were attacked by three communists, dressed in black silk pajamas I took out the first communist with a field goal kicked to his groin while screaming in pain I finished by choking him to death. When I got up, I heard my smallest friend screaming in pain and blood coming down the left side of his head. The enemy had his left earlobe firmly between his teeth and his head and in a chokehold, I came around his back took a full backswing, and uppercut him with all my strength, the sound of the impact was like a crunching sound in his neck, twisted and a strange direction. He hit the ground and started flopping around like a fish out of water. I immediately put a compress on my friend's left ear to stop the bleeding. My other friend was a 1965 Golden Gloves, heavyweight black, golden gloves champion. The last common champion was by the throat using his head like a speed bag. After a short time, he fell, and at last he moved. I reached to my waistband and we drew a half pint of cheap whiskey. We all had a good drink and then proceeded to our base. It was years later I was in bed with my six-year-old grandson. I was awakened by his screaming granddaddy over and over. I woke up at 2 AM. I had my hands around his neck. I told him to go back to sleep, Granddaddy was having a bad dream. I have been on all PTSD medication from 1980 until the day and 2024.

COMMON Sense!!!!!

This is a good tool to direct us to a Successful life

On my first combat appointment to North Vietnam, we were close enough to see red China. We were able to observe many ships carrying supplies to the port in North Vietnam. History will give you information on how to win a war without huge laws on life in the days of great ancient armies, discovered a great, saving tactic common sense tells us that all armies depend on a steady supply of food, shelter, weapons, and medical supplies. The ancient armies would shut down the supply rules. The intermediate result will be the loss of morale and the ability to continue the fight. A sample example of when I was young and admired the large, beautiful hornet nest in the trees. I will take a large, clear plastic bag and enclose the nest at night. I would make sure the bag was airtight after several days of inactivity. I would take down the nest and dump all of the dead hornets, leaving a beautiful nest. I never got stung, by using God-given common sense. JOE FIND A BRAIN!!!

SEPTEMBER 2023

A warning and instrument of and to the nonbelievers of the true book of the law THE HOLY BIBLE the radical members Of the demonic Democrat party this include the number one crime of the syndicate Biden family Mendez family and the entire Biden government in the outhouse white house congress senate fbi doj, all radical left democratic socialist Marxist Followers from the word of God, James, chapter 51 through seven go now you rich man, weep and yell for your misery that shall come upon you. Your riches are corrupted, and your garments are moth-eaten your gold and silver are cankered, and the rest of them shall be a witness against you, and shall eat your flesh as it were fire you have heed treasure together for the last days you have lived in pleasure on the Earth, and been walking you have nourished your heart as in a day of slaughter Dems remember, God made man and woman, Adam, and Eve, not Adam and Steve, please no more White House drag queen parties for your administration my advice to all people who support the demonic democratic party, you better turn before you burn. God said no sin is going to enter in you better turn before you burn in the eternal life of fire, amen and amen! the sin that Joe Biden has added to the world has caused a company called Preparation, H to make Billions and billions of dollars with the cross-dresser cornhole-loving people Joe's transportation man who can't even fix a pothole is now screaming in the White House nightly with his wife or husband whatever I don't know but he keeps hollering that I want to change around here I'm sick and tired of being second fiddle. It's my turn this week to be frank in this relationship. I'm tired of buying all the preparation H.

THE DAY AFTER BIDEN'S GAFF, STUPID ANSWERS, AND FLAT REFUSAL OF POINTED QUESTIONS BY JUMPING TO THE NEXT REPORTER AND THE APPARENT LACK OF MENTAL ACUITY ALL I COULD DO AS I WATCHED WAS LAUGH IN HORROR AND TO MY DISMAY MY LAUGHTER SOUNDED LIKE CAMEL'S SICKENING HORSE LAUGH!! THE ENTIRE MEETING WAS A TOTAL DISASTER FILLED WITH INCOMPLETE AND INCORRECT INFORMATION. THE NEWS THE FOLLOWING DAY SHOULD HAVE BEEN "CLEAN UP ON ASILES 1 THROUGH 99". I DON'T BELIEVE A THOUSAND COWS WITH UPSET STOMACHS EMPTYING THEIR BOWELS ONTO A BALLROOM DANCE FLOOR WOULD HAVE BEEN AS BAD!!!!! I STILL BELIEVE WHEN THE DOCTORS OPERATED ON BIDEN'S COLON THE SMALL ROUND PIECE OF TISSUE THEY FOUND WAS NOT WHAT THEY CLAIMED- RATHER IT WAS THE LAST REMAINING PARTICLE OF BIDEN'S MISSING BRAIN!!!!!! I BELIEVE WHEN BIDEN PASSES THE COUNTRY CAN SAVE A HUGE AMOUNT OF FUNERAL EXPENSES BY GIVING JOE AN ENEMA AND BURY THE REMAINS IN A MATCH BOX!!!!
RIP!!!!!
PSALM 64
HEAR MY VOICE, GOD, IN MY PRAYER;
PRESERVE MY LIFE FROM THE ENEMY.
HIDE ME FROM THE SECRET COUNSEL OF THE WICKED; FROM THE INSURRECTION OF THE WORKERS OF INIQUITY:
WHO WHET THEIR TONGUE LIKE A SWORD, BEND THEIR BOWS TO SHOOT THEIR ARROWS, EVEN BITTER WORDS:
THAT THEY MAY SHOOT IN SECRET AT THE PERFECT: SUDDENLY DO THEY SHOOT AT HIM, AND FEAR NOT.

THEY ENCOURAGE THEMSELVES IN AN EVIL MATTER: THEY COMMUNE OF LAYING SNARES PRIVILY; THEY SAY, WHO SHALL SEE THEM? ANOTHER BIDEN DEMONIC NATIONAL DISASTER !!!

DO YOU EVER WONDER WHAT CAUSED THE GREAT TOILET PAPER SHORTAGE?

THE ANSWER IS THE FACT THAT OUR CLUELESS PRESIDENT HAS MOVED THE ENTIRE WHITE HOUSE TO THE COUNTRY HILLSIDE {OUT HOUSE} IN ONLY 10 MONTHS!!

WHEN THE GEREATIC LEFT POLITICIANS GET MORE FULL OF --IT THE MORE THE DEMAND FOR TOILET PAPER.

BIDEN'S SOLUTION IS TO HAVE CORN FARMERS INCREASE THE SUPPLY OF SILVER QUEEN {SOFT} CORN COBS. THIS WILL RESULT IN A FINANCIAL INCREASE FOR PREP-H OINTMENT SALES.

SLEEPY JOE IS THE #1 PAIN IN THE REAR END!!!! C'MON MAN!!!!!

TODAY IS 11/19/2021 AND IT IS VERY APPARENT WHY YOUR DEMONIC CONGRESS AND SENATE WOULD NOT LET YOU GET A COGNITIVE EXAM!!! YOU COULD MAYBE CHANGE YOUR NUMBERS IF YOU COULD SPEAK ON ANY SUBJECT FOR 10 MIN.

WITHOUT LOOKING AT YOUR TELEPROMPTER FOR A CANNED SPEECH FROM YOUR HANDLERS!!! YOU ARE CLAIMING A FANTASTIC JOB IN ALL AREAS OF YOUR JOB!!!! I AM A 100% DISABLED VET AND I HAVE NOT SEEN ANY OF THE EXCESSIVE

• MONEY TO BUY MORE STUFF THAT YOU ARE BS-ING TO THE PUBLIC. GOD HAS BLESSED THE WORLD WITH MILLIONS OF YEARS OF FOSSIL FUEL! AOC (ABSENCE OF CONSCIENCE) CAN TELL THE WORLD WHEN GREEN NEW GAS WILL PROPEL AIR FORCE 1 AROUND THE WORLD. IT TAKES A TOTAL IMBECILE TO STOP THE OIL SUPPLY FOR 100% OF THIS COUNTRY'S NEEDS PLUS EXPORTS!! AND

BEG OUR ENEMIES FOR OIL!!! WHEN IS THE PROPOSED INVENTION OF ENERGY FOR ALL US AIR FORCE JETS NAVY JETS, AIRCRAFT CARRIERS, etc.? I HAVE NOT SEEN ONE ELECTRIC DELTA JET. JOE YOU WOULD HAVE BETTER LUCK TRYING TO COMMUNICATE WITH THE BUILDERS OF UFOS THAT DON'T USE FOSSIL FUEL!!!! I WILL SURVIVE YOU'RE HELL-BENT ATTEMPT TO DESTROY THE USA!! YOU ENJOY YOUR COMPLETE TURKEY MEAL AND I'LL ENJOY MY MCDONALD 6 PIECE NUGGET AND SMALL FRENCH FRY DINNER!! BUT DUE TO YOUR INEPT GAS BLUNDER, I WILL HAVE TO WALK TO MCDONALDS!!!

SUPER FAKE NEWS!!!!!
WHERE IS THE GLOBAL WARMING TODAY JOE? C'MON MAN!!!!!
JAN 28,2022
JOE PLEASE GIVE US BACK OUR NATURAL GAS AND OIL TO KEEP US WARM I HAVE BURNED THE LAST OF MY FURNITURE TO KEEP THE KIDS WARM!!!!!
RISE O'KEEPER OF THE SUNSHINE, RUSH TO OUR RESCUE Oh-GREAT KEEPER OF THE ATMOSPHERE! WHERE ARE YOU HIDING O-GREAT WORLD THERMOSTAT? YES, YOU OH KEEPER OF THE WORLD HEAT!!!!
AOC APPEARS BEFORE WE ALL FREEZE TO DEATH IN THIS HUGE WINTER STORM. 12 INCHES OF SNOW IN NEW YORK CITY!!!!! THE CITIZENS OF NEW YORK ARE BRACING FOR MAYBE 2 FEET OF FROZEN HEAT!!!!
SUPPLY THEM WITH HEATING OIL TO KEEP WARM AND COOK HOT MEALS!!
THE BIDEN'S HAVE A SECRET IN TIMES LIKE THESE TO KEEP HOT!! WHEN A COLD FORECAST ARRIVES THE ENTIRE BIDEN FAMILY INC. GO TO THEIR FAVORITE SUPER HOT MEXICAN RESTAURANT AND ORDER THE HOTTEST, SPICY FOOD AND EAT UP THEIR FILL! THEN THEY USE THEIR SECRET. THEY ALL EAT A GREAT HELPING OF ICE

CREAM FOR DESSERT AND FOR A FIRE EXTINGUISHER. WHEN THEIR BOWELS START TO RUMBLE THEY ALL RUN TO THEIR THRONES AND SCREAM "COME ON ICE CREAM", SPEAK OH LIPS OF FIRE, OH TOOTHLESS WONDER. COME ON ICE CREAM AND COOL THE FLAMES!
JOE CONTINUE TO TAKE YOUR GAS TO FRANCE AND DROP IT ON THE WORLD STAGE!!!!! THE PYTHONS IN MIAMI WILL BE FALLING FROM THE TREES AGAIN, NOT SINCE OBAMA WAS IN CHARGE!!!!

Sold the farm
OLD MACDONALD HAD A FARM CALLED THE USA. WITH A BRAIN-DEAD JACKASS MULE NAMED JOE EI-EI-O. JACKASS JOE SOLD THE FARM TO THE TALIBAN. SILENT NIGHT-DIE OF FRIGHT!!!!!!
EI—EI—O.

WITH THE SUPPLY CHAIN SUFFERING BIDEN CONSTIPATION! (BRAIN FREEZE TO MUCH ICE CREAM AND THE (CHINA VIRUS} TRUMP WAS RIGHT AGAIN!!! HIGHEST INFLATION IN 30 YEARS, NO GAS OR HEATING OIL OUR (NOT MINE) INCOMPETENT FEARLESS LEADER GAVE A MULTI-BILLION TRUMP APPROVED OIL PIPELINE BY WHICH THE USA WOULD SUPPLY OUR ALLIES AT THAT TIME! A GREAT EARLY CHRISTMAS FOR ONE OF JOE'S A-HOLE FRIENDS!!!!!
C'MON JOE GIVE THE USA A BREAK!!!
PUTIN BUY YOURSELF ANOTHER STALLION!!!!

THE STORY KEEPS COMING!!!
BIMBO BIDEN HANDED OFF THE MANTLE TO THE #2 MOST INCOMPETENT LEADER OF THE UNCONSCIOUS DEMONIC PARTY!
WHILE BIMBO WAS UNDERGOING EXPLORATORY SURGERY THE MEDICAL TEAM MADE A SURPRISING

DISCOVERY!! THEY FOUND THE LAST REMAINING PARTICLE OF BIDENS LOST BALL IN HIGH WEEDS BRAIN II! THE DRS. DESCRIBED IT AS A SMALL BALL ABOUT THE SIZE OF A GREEN PEA! THEY ALSO DISCOVERED A THOUSAND-YEAR SUPPLY OF AOC'S GREEN NEW GAS!!!! THIS CAN SAVE THE TAXPAYERS OF THE USA MILLIONS OF DOLLARS OF FUEL TO FLY THE BIDENS ALL AROUND THE WORLD. SIMPLY TIE JOE TO THE REAR OF AIR FORCE ONE EXPEL ONE OF HIS WORLD-FAMOUS REAR EXPLOSIONS AND PROPEL AF-1 TO SPEEDS ABOVE THE SPEED OF SOUND ANYWHERE IN THE WORLD!!!!

JOHN KERRY EAT YOUR HEART OUT!!! NOW JOE HAS AN ANSWER TO WHY HE COULD NOT MAKE ONE CORRECT MILITARY DECISION IN THE LAST 40 YEARS. NOW JOE IS RESTING IN HIS BEACH BUNKER AND WAS HEARD SINGING HIS FAVORITE SONG TO THE SQUAD AND PUTIN AND XI PING —I'LL DO ANYTHING THAT YOU WANT ME TO - I'M YOUR PUPPET !!!! GOD, PLEASE PUT THE RUNAWAY TRAIN BACK ON THE TRACK IN SEPT. 2022!! PUT THE ADULTS BACK IN CHARGE AND AMERICA FIRST AGAIN!!!! ONLY JESUS CHRIST CAN SAVE US!!!!

THE NEARLY FROZEN BIG GATOR!!

AOC- PLEASE OPEN YOUR BIG MOUTH AND SPEAK VOLUMES

OF HOT AIR!!!!!!

SLEEPY JOE BIDEN LOVES OUR ALLIES?

OUR OLDEST ALLY IS NOT TOO HAPPY WITH BIMBO WITHDRAWING OUR TROOPS IN THE MIDDLE OF THE NIGHT WITHOUT NOTIFYING OUR ALLIES IN AFGHANISTAN! TO RUB MORE SA IN THE WOUND JOE {SUBMARINED} MACRON AGAIN! FRANCE WAS WORKING ON A NUCLEAR SUB-DEAL WITH AUSTRALIA WORTH BILLIONS OF DOLLARS FOR FRANCE! SNEAKY JOE SCOOPED YOU WITH HIS GREEDY DEAL!! GOTCHA AGAIN BUDDY!

NO MORE FREE PERFUME JILL!! WHAT'S THE DANG DEAL
MACAROON? WHERE'S THE {LOVE}
C'MON MAN !!!!

JOE BIDEN WILL BE FOREVER REMEMBERED AS THE MOST
INEPT PERFORMING, CLUELESS, SLEEPY, GAS-FILLED
LEADER IN THE ENTIRE WORLD!!!!
C-MON MAN!! YOU WERE FREE TO THE WORLD WITH
(YOUR) GAS!!
WHAT ABOUT YOURS, IT'S THE HIGHEST IN HISTORY DUE
ONLY TO YOUR BROKEN POLICIES!!!!
C; MON MAN !!!!!!!!!!!

WITH THE SUPPLY CHAIN SUFFERING BIDEN
CONSTIPATION! (BRAIN FREEZE TO MUCH ICE CREAM!
AND THE (CHINA VIRUS) TRUMP WAS RIGHT AGAIN!!!
HIGHEST INFLATION IN
30 YEARS, NO GAS OR HEATING OIL OUR (NOT MINE)
INCOMPETENT FEARLESS LEADER GAVE A MULTI-BILLION
TRUMP APPROVED OIL PIPELINE BY WHICH THE USA
WOULD SUPPLY OUR ALLIES AT THAT TIME! A GR
EARLY CHRISTMAS FOR ONE OF JOE'S A-HOLE FRIENDS!!!!!
C'MON JOE GIVE THE USA A BREAK!!!!
PUTIN BUY YOURSELF ANOTHER STALLION!!!!

REAL CLIMATE FACT!!!!
THE NATIONAL WEATHER FORECASTERS PREDICT
THE WINTER OF 2021 WILL BE BRUTALLY COLD IN THE
NORTH. BURN YOUR FURNITURE SINCE HAPPY UNCLE
JOE IS PLANNING TO SHUT DOWN PIPELINE #5 WHICH
SUPPLIES MOST OF THE NORTH EAST. I DON'T BELIEVE
AOC'S SOLAR PANELS AND BIRD-KILLING WINDMILLS
WILL KEEP YOU AND YOUR FAMILY WARM!!!!! IT'S GOING
TO BE EXTREMELY COLD UP THERE---AOC WHERE IS THE
DANGEROUS HEAT WAVE? GREEN NEW GAS WILL NOT

SAVE YOU! NEITHER WILL JOE ABUNDANCE OF GAS!!!!!
MY BEST IS TO PRAY FOR SOMEONE IN THE WHITE HOUSE
WILL STUMBLE UPON A "BRAIN" I DON'T THINK IT'S
POSSIBLE!!!!

I HAVE HEARD THAT YOUR RADICAL MARXIST SOCIALIST
PARTY MEMBERS SAY ON NATIONAL TV THEY DON'T
HAVE A MAGIC WAND TO STOP THE HIGH GAS PRICES!!!!
BUT SHE WAS ABLE TO GIVE A BIG VP HORSE LAUGH !!
KUDOS
PLEASE LET MY 9-YEAR-OLD GRANDSON GIVE TO YOU A
FANTASTIC SOLUTION TO THE PROBLEM!!!! SIMPLY PULL
YOUR HEAD OUT OF YOUR REAR END AND RECIND
EVERY EX. ORDER YOU CANCELED FROM THE GREATEST
PRESIDENT EVER. THE TRUMPSTER!!!!
C'MON MAN GET WITH THE PROGRAM!!!!

I THINK AOC SHOULD LEAVE POLITICS AND GO TO
ADVERTISING!!
SHE THINKS ALL REPUBLICAN POLITICIANS WANT TO
DATE HER! I THINK SHE COULD MAKE A FORTUNE IF
SHE WORKED FOR A MAGAZINE THAT PROMOTED THE
SALE OF VIAGRA. SHE COULD PUT ON A HEAVY COAT OF
BRIGHT RED LIP GLOSS AND APPEAR TO BE BLOWING A
BIG KISS TO ALL THE MEN OF THE WORLD! THIS COULD
STOP THE CURRENT GLOBAL FREEZING GOING ON NOW!!
HER RED LIPS WOULD RAISE THE DEGREE OF THE HEAT
OF THE MEAT FOR MOST MEN!! NO PUN INTENDED!!
IT MIGHT EVEN WORK FOR SOME EMPLOYEES AT CNN!
PLEASE HURRY I'M FREEZING DURING THIS GLOBAL
WARMING HERE IN SOUTH FLORIDA!!
ANY COMPLAINTS MAY CONTACT ME AT (407-SIX-NINE-OH
-EIGHT
ONE TOO!!!!!! THE BIG GATOR!!!

2024 THE TIME IS HERE TO PUT A SUPERMAN BACK IN CHARGE OF THE "OUT HOUSE WHITE HOUSE" AND IN CHARGE OF THE USA AND THE WORLD!!!! BARRACK DREW RED LINES IN THE SANDS OF ALL OF OUR ENEMIES THEN SAT BACK AND CHEWED HIS TONGUE AND SILENTLY WATCHED OUR ENEMIES BLOW THE RED LINES AWAY!!! NO ONE WANTED TO GIVE CREDIT TO THE BRAVEST, MOST INTELLIGENT LEADER TO EVER WALK ON THE EARTH!!!!! THE ORANGE MAN WAS THE BEST DR. IN HISTORY TOO! WHEN HE TOOK OFFICE HE IMMEDIATELY CASTRATED PUTIN, CHI PING, NORTH KOREAN FAT BOY, AND THE GOD HATING RAG HEAD IN IRAN!! AND THE AFGHANISTAN RAG HEAD LEADER. THE RED LINES FROM TRUMP WERE MESS WITH THE USA AND "WILL BLOW YOUR DUMB BEHINDS OFF THE MAP !!! IN JAN .2025 TRUMP WILL MAKE AMERICA GREAT AGAIN, ENERGY EFFICIENT #1 SUPPLIER OF CLEAN ENERGY TO THE WORLD!! DURING TRUMP ERA STUDENTS IN THE 5TH. GRADE COULD SCHOOL WORK ON 8TH GRADE LEVEL. UNDER BIMBO BIDEN'S GENDER EDUCATION LEADER OUR SCHOOLS ARE LOWER RATED WORLDWIDE THAN ALL 3RD WORLD COUNTRIES.

BIMBOS TRANSPORTATION SWEETIE COULD NOT BLOW 4 5-YEAR-OLD POPSICLE STICK BOAT ACROSS THE BATHTUB MUCH LESS GET TRUCKS, BOATS, OR LANES NOW TRAINS FROM ONE STATE TO ANOTHER!!!!

ERICA LOVES JOE DRAG QUEEN KID SHOWS AND BEAUTIFUL LUGGAGE STEALING NUCLEAR WASTE GURU CAKE SAMMY. HE WAS PRAYING FOR JAIL TIME IN L MALE JAIL-AKA TRANS MAN HEAVEN!!!! AND A LIFE SUPPLY OF "PREP-H". SPEAK O-LIPS-OF-FIRE.

OH, TOOTHLESS WONDER!!!!!

C'MON MAN!!!!!|

TODAY IS 11/19/2021 AND IT IS VERY APPARENT WHY YOUR DEMONIC CONGRESS AND SENATE WOULD NOT LET YOU

GET A COGNITIVE EXAM!!! YOU COULD MAYBE CHANGE YOUR NUMBERS IF YOU COULD SPEAK ON ANY SUBJECT FOR 10 MIN.

WITHOUT LOOKING AT YOUR TELEPROMPTER FOR A CANNED SPEECH FROM YOUR HANDLERS!!! YOU ARE CLAIMING A FANTASTIC JOB IN ALL AREAS OF YOUR JOB!!! I AM A 100% DISABLED VET AND I HAVE NOT SEEN ANY OF THE EXCESSIVE MONEY TO BUY MORE STUFF THAT YOU ARE BS-ING TO THE PUBLIC. GOD HAS BLESSED THE WORLD WITH MILLIONS OF YEARS OF FOSSIL FUEL! AOC (ABSENCE OF CONSCIENCE) CAN TELL THE WORLD WHEN GREEN NEW GAS WILL PROPEL AIR FORCE 1 AROUND THE WORLD. IT TAKES A TOTAL IMBECILE TO STOP THE OIL SUPPLY FOR 100% OF THIS COUNTRY'S NEEDS PLUS EXPORTS!! AND BEG OUR ENEMIES FOR OIL!!! WHEN IS THE PROPOSED INVENTION OF ENERGY FOR ALL US AIR FORCE JETS NAVY JETS, AIRCRAFT CARRIERS ETC.? I HAVE NOT SEEN ONE ELECTRIC DELTA JET. JOE YOU WOULD HAVE BETTER LUCK TRYING TO COMMUNICATE WITH THE BUILDERS OF UFOS THAT DON'T USE FOSSIL FUEL!!!! I WILL SURVIVE YOUR HELL-BENT ATTEMPT TO DESTROY THE USA!! YOU ENJOY YOUR COMPLETE TURKEY MEAL AND I'LL ENJOY MY MCDONALD 6 PIECE NUGGET AND SMALL FRENCH FRY DINNER!! BUT DUE TO YOUR INEPT GAS BLUNDER, I WILL HAVE TO WALK TO MCDONALDS!!!

BY THE WAY, I WITNESSED UFOS OFF THE COAST OF N. VIET NAM. THEY WERE VERY IMPRESSIVE, FAST AS A LIGHTNING BOLT AND LEAVING NO SMOKE TRAIL, I WAS THERE FROM 1966 TO 1969.

JOE DON'T EXPOSE YOUR DINNER GUEST TO A CLOUD OF YOUR GREEN NEW GAS!! I WISH ALL CITIZENS LIVING ON A FIXED INCOME "HAPPY THANKSGIVING" BY THE WAY IT MIGHT BE POSSIBLE TO GET A SMALL LOAN FROM THE SOON-TO-BE WEALTHY ILLEGAL IMMIGRANTS!!!!

YEA!! MONEY FOR THEE NOT FOR ME!!!! ALL MADE POSSIBLE BY THE ENTIRE BRAIN DEAD DEMONIC BIDEN ADMINISTRATION!!!!!

JUSTICE IN AMERICA? P?
DURING THE RIOTS IN 2929 THE LEFT DEMS NEVER MADE SOUND TO STOP BT TE WOTIF 1AA US
GOT TOGETHER WITH BILLIONAIRE DEMOCRATS TO SET UP FUND PROGRAMS TO GET FELON RIOTERS WHO ATTACKED GOVERNMENT OFFICES IMMEDIATELY OUT OF JAIL TO RIOT AGAIN!
I GUESS I HAVE BEEN MISINFORMED ALL OF MY LIFE THAT OUR ELECTED OFFICIALS ARE ELECTED TO UPHOLD THE CONSTITUTION OF THE USA!!
WE CAN BUILD A $450.000 WALL AROUND BIDEN'S BEACH HOUSE BUT NOT BUILD THE ALREADY PAID-FOR BORDER WALL, IS JOE'S BEHIND MADE OF SILVER AND GOLD, AND ALL AMERICANS ARE MADE OF RUST! OUR LIVES ARE VALUABLE ALSO!!! NOW IN 2021, THE LEADER OF THE BLM IS TELLING THE INCOMING MAYOR IF HE PUTS THE POLICE BACK IN THE "HOOD" AND ARRESTS CRIMINALS THERE WILL BE RIOTING FIRES, AND BLOODSHED!!! WHERE ARE OUR SO CALLED LEADERS?? LEADERS IN NAME ONLY!!!!! BEWARE OF YOUR BEHINDS IN 2022!!!!

I BELIEVE I OWE OUR BRAIN-DEAD PRESIDENT AN APOLOGY!!!
IT CAME TO ME THIS MORNING THAT OUR
MARXIST, COMMUNIST, SOCIALIST, RADICAL LEFT ISLAMIC LOVING PRE-RUNNER OF THE ANTICHRIST LEADER HAD A HIDDEN PLAN ALL THE TIME!!!! IF YOU WANT TO TURN THE FAUCI-CLAIMED OBESE POPULATION FOR THE COVID-19 SPREAD, JOE HAS DEVELOPED A CURE!!! TAKE GAS AWAY FROM AMERICANS AND MAKE THEM WALK EVERYWHERE THEY GO!

CREATE A SUPPLY SHORTAGE OF ALL PHYSICAL NEEDS. BABY FORMULA, GROCERIES, BREAD ETC. DO NOT INTERFERE WITH QUEEN NANCY'S $ 25-A-PINT ICE CREAM OR WHATEVER KEEPS JERRY NADLER'S BARREL BELLY BLOWN UP!! BY WALKING 7

DAYS A WEEK AND EATING GRASS WE WILL BECOME A NEW NATION OF STARVED NATIONS IN AFRICA. BIG BELLIES-ARMS AND LEGS LIKE STICKS!!! FARMERS WILL NO LONGER NEED FERTILIZER TO GROW CROPS TO ROT IN THE FIELDS TRANSPORTATION. AMERICA WILL BE HEALTHY AND NOT WEALTHY!!! WHAT A GREAT SECRET PLAN TO BUILD BACK BETTER!!!!! SAVE THE WORLD VOTE INTELLIGENCE IN 2024!!!!

REPUBLICAN LIFESAVER DONALD TRUMP, PRESIDENT IN 2024!!! DRIVE AND EAT AGAIN!!!!!!

I SPOKE TOO SOON!! BIDEN STUPIDY EXPOSED AGAIN!! THE DEMONIC LEFT CLAIMS THEY DON'T HAVE ENOUGH MONEY TO PROTECT OUR SCHOOLS!!!! EXPOSED TODAY--THE GOVT IS PAYING THE CONTRACTORS WHO HAVE BEEN PAID ALREADY TO BUILD THE WALL AND THE MATERIAL IS PAID FOR!! BIMBO

IS PAYING THE CONTRACTOR 1 MILLION A DAY (365 MILLION A YEAR TO GUARD THE PAID-FOR FENCE IN THE DESERT!!!! HOW MANY SCHOOLS CAN BE SECURED WITH THIS WASTED MONEY!!! THE ENTIRE DEMOCRATIC PARTY NEEDS TO PULL THEIR BRAIN-DEAD HEADS OUT OF THEIR REAR ENDS!!!!!

BILLIONS GIVEN TO CROOKS IN STIMULUS FRAUD!!! PUT A NEW CRACK PIPE KIT IN EVERY DEMOCRAT CHRISTMAS STOCKING!!!!! JOE IS GOING DOWN IN A TOILET BOWL WHIRLPOOL !!!!! GO JOE GO!! AROUND THE BOWL AND DOWN THE HOLE!!!!! FORGET ROE V WADE-ABORT JOE NOW!!!!!

ANYONE WHO DOES NOT LIKE THIS TWEET MAY CALL

1-407-69-0000H-U812! THE WARNING IS OUT!!! IT IS TIME FOR EVERYONE TO EXAMINE THEIR LIVES AND THE WAY THEY'RE LIVING AND IF THEIR LIVES ARE NOT PLEASING IN THE SIGHT OF GOD YOU BETTER TURN BEFORE YOU BURN!!!!

BYE BYE ANTICHRIST JOE, CRAZY NANCY, AND ALL RADICAL LEFT DEMONCTRATS. I WILL MISS YOU ALL LIKE THE REMOVAL OF AN INFECTED BOIL ON TOP OF A HEMORRHOID!!! NO MORE PAIN IN THE BEHIND OR THE WALLET!!!!!!
RELIEF AT LAST "HELLO DONALD TRUMP"

BIDEN ELECTRICIANS!!!!
HOW MANY DEMOCRATS DOES IT TAKE TO INSTALL A CEILING LIGHT BULB?????
ANSWER ----3 --- ONE TO HOLD THE LIGHT BULB AND 2 TO TURN THE LADDER!!!!!!!

FAA NORTHERN TRIANGLE ALERT!!!!
STRANGE LOOKING BORDER
CZAR PATROLLING 60,000
MIGRANTS HEADING TOWARDS THE USA! CZAR VP SEEN FLYING ON A GREEN NEW GAS-POWERED BROOM!!!
LOTS OF HORSES LAUGHING BUT
NO SOLUTIONS OFFERED.
IT'S A BIRD-IT'S A PLANE-NO
IT'S A FLYING HORSE
LAUGHING VP---GO CAMEL-AH

PAYBACK PENALTIES FOR BIMBO BIDENS MANDATORY VACCINATIONS:
ANYONE WHO CAN PROVE NEGATIVE REACTION FROM FORCED VACCINATION WILL BE

PAID $100,000 FROM THE BIDEN ADMIN. ANY WHO DIED AS A RESULT OF THE SHOT THEIR FAMILY WILL BE PAID ONE MILLION FROM THE BIDEN FAMILY ACCOUNT. PAY YOUR FAIR SHARE JOE!!!!!

A GIANT C-116 AIR FORCE PLANE WITH OVER 200 AFGHANS ON BOARD CRASHED ON A MOUNTAINTOP ON THE BORDER OF AFGHANISTAN AND PAKISTAN. MEANWHILE, SLEEPY JOE WHO WAS ON VACATION AGAIN LAY PONDERING WHICH SIDE OF THE BORDER TO BURY THE SURVIVORS!!!!!!!

ROOT CAUSES DISCOVERED!!!
MY 8-YEAR-OLD MODERATELY MENTALLY HANDICAPPED SON DISCOVERED THE TOTAL ROOT CAUSES OF THE COLLAPSE OF THE SOUTHERN BORDER!!!!!!
1600 PENNSYLVANIA AVE!!!!!!

JOE BIDEN!!!!
PLEASE TAKE OFF YOUR EYE MASK AND YOUR C-PAP BEFORE YOU MAKE ANY MORE OVER THE HORIZON DEADLY DECISIONS!!!!!!

JOE'S BATTLE CRY
HANG DOWN YOUR HEADS ALL HOSTAGES, HANG DOWN YOUR HEADS AND CRY. HANG DOWN YOUR HEADS ALL HOSTAGES -
TALIBAN LEADER ABDULLAH
SAYS ALL OF YOU ARE GOING TO DIE!!!! COURTESY OF DEMONIC DEMOCRATIC LEADER BRAIN DEAD JOE BIDEN!!

THE BIDEN ADMINISTRATION LUST FOR POWER AT THE COST OF THE NATION.
"I WANT IT ALL AND I WANT IT NOW !!!!

THE BIBLE SAYS YOU CAN SWALLOW A CAMEL [THE WANTS OF THEIR GREEDY PARTY] BUT THEY CHOKE ON A GNAT [THE NEEDS OF THE PEOPLE] LOSE IT ALL OVER A LITTLE LOSS!
THERE WAS A LITTLE DOG NAMED JOE WHO LIVED IN A TRAIN YARD. ONE DAY A TRAIN FULL OF POWER AND FAME CAME BY AND JOE RAN IN FRONT OF THE TRAIN [AKA] THE DEM PARTY. JOE WAS SLOW AND THE TRAIN CUT OFF A SMALL PIECE OF JOES TAIL [EGO]. JOE RAN BACK ACROSS THE TRACK TO RETRIEVE HIS EGO AND THE TRAIN CUT OFF HIS HEAD. THE MORAL OF THE STORY IS DON'T LOSE YOUR HEAD OVER A LITTLE PIECE OF TAIL [EGO.] A LESSON FOR ALL; POWER IS SUPPOSED TO BE FOR ALL THE MASSES NOT THE ASSES [DEMONSTRATES]

"EQUAL EDUCATION"??????
HAVE YOU EVER HEARD THE PHRASE "A MIND IS TERRIBLE THING TO WASTE?
UNDER THE CURRENT ADMINISTRATION
EDUCATION IS STILL BEING REFUSED TO THE MINORITY INNER CITY POPULATION. DONALD TRUMP WAS A STRONG PROPONENT OF SCHOOL CHOICE WHICH WOULD AFFORD INNER-CITY CHILDREN WOULD BE ABLE TO RECEIVE AN EQUAL EDUCATION UNDER THE LAW. CRT IS A TOOL OF THE LEFT TO IGNITE MORE DISCRIMINATION IN THIS COUNTRY. IN A RECENT CONVERSATION I HAD A STRANGER IN MY NEIGHBORHOOD. HIS BEST FRIEND (BLACK) AND HIS (WHITE) WIFE HAVE A BLACK DAUGHTER, THEY NOTICED THEIR DAUGHTER WAS ANGRY AFTER SCHOOL!
SHE STATED SHE HATED HER MOTHER BECAUSE SHE WAS WHITE! THE YOUNG GIRL WAS TOLD

IN SCHOOL SHE WOULD NEVER REACH SUCCESS IN LIFE BECAUSE SHE WAS BLACK! THANKS TO BIMBO BIDENS

PICK FOR ATTORNEY GENERAL WHOSE SON-IN-LAW WAS PROMOTING CRITICAL RACE THEORY!!!! REMEMBER JOE AND KKK BYRD TRIED TO STOP SCHOOL BUSING SO JOES CHILDREN WOULD NOT BE TAUGHT IN A "RACIAL JUNGLE", BLOW THE DOG WHISTLE JOE". WE NEED TO PASS SCHOOL CHOICE TO GIVE ALL CHILDREN AN EQUAL CHANCE AT SUCCESS IN THE USA!! STOP EDUCATION FOR "ME" NOT FOR THEE!!!!!

WOW!!!! WHAT A GREAT DECISION TO STOP DRILLING FOR MORE OIL WHEN THE BURNING-UP ATMOSPHERE IS EXPECTED TO HAVE A VERY COLD WINTER AND INFLATION IS GETTING OUT OF CONTROL, WAGES ARE GETTING EATEN ALIVE THEY ARE GOING DOWN BECAUSE INFLATION HAS OUTGAINED AND WIPED OUT ALL GAINS IN WAGES!!!!!
GREAT IDEA!!!! WIPE OUT FOSSIL FUEL NOW!!!
WHAT GREAT SOLUTION DOES AOC HAVE FOR THE AIRLINE INDUSTRY???? I HAVE NOT SEEN ANY SOLAR OR WIND-POWERED AIRPLANES YET !! ONLY VP'S AMAZING GREEN NEW GAS POWERED BROOM!!!!! WHERE WOULD THE WORLD BE NOW IF THEY SHOT ALL THE HORSES TO PULL THE WAGONS BEFORE THEY INVENTED GAS-POWERED AUTOS ??? HOW ABOUT JOE'S 85-CAR CONVOY AND A WAVE OF CARBON-SPEWING KERRY PRIVATE JETS. NANCY SAYS (GAS FOR ME!!!! NOT FOR THEE!!!!) NANCY DO YOU HAVE YOUR OWN SOLAR POWERED HAIR DRYER??? JUST OPEN YOUR MOUTH AND LET THE HOT AIR DO THE JOB!!! YOU ALWAYS USE SOME OF JOE BIDEN 'S REAR END GAS!!!

TO WRAP THIS JOURNEY ALL UP I WANT TO REMIND READERS THAT I AM NOT A RADICAL PERSON BUT I FIRMLY BELIEVE IF THE RADICAL BIDEN ADMINISTRATION CONTINUES ON ITS DESTRUCTIVE WAY THERE WILL BE

ANOTHER DESTRUCTIVE WAR BETWEEN THE RADICAL LEFT STATES AND THE SEEKERS OF LAW AND ORDER AND A GOVERNMENT BY AND FOR THE PEOPLE OF THE ONCE MOST POWERFUL AND RESPECTED NATION IN THE WORLD. IN ONLY 10 SHORT MONTHS WE HAVE FALLEN FROM #1 MILITARY TO #3 OR #4. WE HAVE LOST THE RESPECT OF OUR MOST RELIABLE ALLIES. OUR BORDERS ARE THE MOST WIDELY DESTRUCTIVE AND DEPLORABLE IN THE WORLD JOE SURVIVES GOD BLESS THE USA (RIP)!!!!!

GOD'S WARNING TO THE DEMONIC BIDEN ADMINISTRATION
PSALM 64
HEAR MY VOICE OF GOD, IN MY PRAYER;
PRESERVE MY LIFE FROM THE ENEMY.
HIDE ME FROM THE SECRET COUNSEL OF THE WICKED; FROM THE INSURRECTION OF THE WORKERS OF INIQUITY:
WHO WHET THEIR TONGUE LIKE A SWORD, BEND THEIR BOWS TO SHOOT THEIR ARROWS, EVEN BITTER WORDS: THAT THEY MAY SHOOT IN SECRET AT THE PERFECT: SUDDENLY DO THEY SHOOT AT HIM, AND FEAR NOT.
THEY ENCOURAGE THEMSELVES IN AN EVIL MATTER: THEY COMMUNE OF LAYING SNARES
PRIVILY; THEY SAY, WHO SHALL SEE THEM?

THE INFORMATION CONTAINED IS BASED ON THE BELIEFS AND KNOWLEDGE OF THE WRITER DERIVED FROM SELF-OBTAINED KNOWLEDGE AND INFORMATION FROM CORRECT AND TRUE NEWS OUTLETS AND STORIES FROM FAKE NEWS
BROADCAST!! I BELIEVE THAT PERSON IN THE WHITE HOUSE IS THE FORERUNNER OF THE ANTICHRIST AND THE PROMOTER OF THE MARK OF THE BEAST!! THE MARK IS THE (D) FOR DEMONIC-DEMOCRAT. WITH THE

MARK YOU CAN BUY THE OUT OF THE WORLD CRACK-PIPE PAINTINGS WITHOUT EXPOSING YOUR IDENTITY. I HOPE IF THIS BOOK SELLS FOR LESS THAN $400,000 IN A YEAR, I WILL NOT PAY TAXES LIKE THE "PAINTER". I BELIEVE GOD IS IN CHARGE OF THE CLIMATE NOT RADICAL DEMS!!! I NEARLY FROZE TO DEATH DURING THE GLOBAL WARMING- RETURN OF THE "ICE AGE" 2022-2023 SEASON. IT WAS SAID IF JOE BIDEN WAS IN CHARGE OF THE DESERTS OF THE WORLD, THEY WOULD RUN OUT OF SAND! IF IN CHARGE OF THE OCEANS THERE WOULD BE NO SEA LIFE SINCE JOE WOULD DRAIN THE WATERS OF THE WORLD!!!!! MY PRAYER FOR THE WORLD IS THAT GOD WILL PUT A LEADER BACK IN OFFICE TO (MAKE AMERICA GRE AGAIN). JOE WHATEVER YOU SAY OR DO IN DARKNESS WILL BE HEARD IN THE LIGHT AND SHOUTED FROM THE ROOFTOPS!!! AMEN!!
RESPECTFULLY THE BIG "RED, WHITE, AND BLUE GATOR!!!!!

WHO IS THE REAL JOE B.?? AKA ROBERT PETERS-AKA ROBERT WARE OR JRB WARE? WILL THE REAL BIMBO BIDEN PLEASE STAND UP!!!! JOE BIDEN IS THE REAL BIG GUY, HEAD OF THE BIDEN (RICO) CRIME SYNDICATE FAMILY!!! JOE YOU LAUGH WHEN SOMEONE SAYS (WHERE'S THE MONEY HOW ABOUT OVER 100 BANK INQUIRIES NOT VERIFIED? HOW MANY OFF-SHORE BANK ACCOUNTS DO YOU HAVE? A WORD TO THE WISE JOEY BABY!! IT IS ALWAYS BETTER TO KEEP YOUR MOUTH CLOSED AND LET PEOPLE THINK YOU ARE STUPID- DON'T OPEN YOUR MOUTH WIDE AND PROVE YOU ARE!!! EVERY DAY ANOTHER LAYER OF THE BIDEN ``RICO" SYNDICATE FAMILY ONION IS BEING PEELED AWAY! ELECTION INTERFERENCE BY TRUMP "MY ASS!!' I HAVE VIDEO RECORDINGS OF STACY ABRAHAMS CONFRONTING GOV. KEMP SHOUTING HE RIGGED THE ELECTIONS!!!! RICO FOR REPUBLICANS, BUT

NOT FOR DEMONIC DEMOCRATS!!! BIMBO, YOU HAVE
SINGLE-HANDEDLY TOTALLY CORRUPTED THE DEPT OF
JUSTICE FBI AND DESTROYED THE ENTIRE US ECONOMY
WITH BIDEN-DEMONICS!! RUINED THE #1 MILITARY IN
THE WORLD!! DESTROYED THE EDUCATION SYSTEM
FOR ALL AMERICAN CHILDREN!!! DESTROYED THE
TRANSPORTATION IN LAND SEA AND AIR WITH CORN
HOLE PETE CAN'T EVEN FIX A POTHOLE!!!! IS IT STRANGE.
EVERY CASE OF RICO IS BY RADICAL DEM
BILLIONAIRE GEORGE SOROS PAID TO HAVE ALL
DUMB-ASSED DAS BEG TO PROSECUTE YOUR ONLY REP.
CHALLENGER!!
WHEN IS YOUR NEXT SCHEDULED DRAG QUEEN PARTY
AT THE NOW OUT-HOUSE WHITE-HOUSE?
BE SURE TO INVITE ALL OF YOUR SWEETIE HAPPY
CABINET DRESSED IN BEAUTIFUL PINK DRESSES AND
SPANDEX!!!! JUST WHAT AMERICAN CHILDREN NEED TO
SEE!!!! OPEN THE GATES OF (HELL)!! TRY INVITING ADAM
AND EVE -NOT PETIE AND SAMMY!!!
GOD BLESS THE USA IN 2025-"MAKE AMERICA GREAT
AGAIN!!!!" WHAT ABOUT YOUR SOUTHERN BORDER AND
YOUR BRAINLESS 2-BORDER
CZARS!! OVER 5 MILLION ILLEGAL CRIMINALS AND DRUG
DEALERS WALKING INTO AMERICA WITH A JOE BIDEN
CELL PHONE!!!! DON'T FORGET YOUR DAY LATE-DOLLAR
SHORT VACATION TO HAWAII.
WHAT A POWERFUL OFFER!!!! $700.00 TO ALL FAMILIES
THAT LOST EVERYTHING INCLUDING FAMILY MEMBERS!!!!
WHAT A WORTHLESS DISPLAY OF SYMPATHY!! I BET YOU
MOVED THE ROAD WHEN YOU SAID YOU ALMOST LOST
OUR CORVETTE IN A FIRE THAT NEVER REACHED UR
HOUSE!! DID YOUR RESPONSE TEAM DERS ENJOY THEIR
NIGHTS IN $1200.A NIGH EL ROOMS?? JOE DID YOU FIND
ANY YOUNG.

GIRLS THAT DID NOT HAVE THEIR HAIR BURNT OFF!! IF YOU EVER TRIED TO SMELL MY GRANDDAUGHTER'S HAIR YOUR NOSE WOULD BE IN THE BACK OF YOUR HEAD!!!!! START PAYING AMERICAN CITIZENS MONEY FOR FOOD, CLOTHING, HOUSING AND MEDICINE. QUIT PAYING CHINA FOR ALL ILLEGAL DRUGS!

FINALLY FOR YOU JOE! THERE WAS A TIME IN MY LIFE WHEN I HAD ONE FOOT ON A BANANA PEEL AND ONE FOOT IN THE GRAVE!!!!

MY WIFE MADE ME TURN TO GOD!!! ONE NIGHT ABOUT 2:00 AM 1 WAS READING MY BIBLE AND I HEARD A VERY LOUD VOICE TELLING ME TO STOP READING AND LISTEN! I ASKED MY WIFE IF SHE HEARD THE VOICE AND SHE REPLIED NO. I JUST SAT STILL FOR A WHILE THEN PICKED UP MY BIBLE AND BEGAN READING AGAIN. SUDDENLY THE VOICE RETURNED LOUDER THAN BEFORE AND SAID THE END IS NEAR AND IT'S TIME FOR EVERYONE TO EXAMINE THEIR LIFE AND LIFESTYLES AND IF THE LIVES THEY WERE LIVING WERE NOT PLEASING IN THE SIGHT OF GOD!! AND IF YOU WANT TO GO TO HEAVEN ONE DAY YOU MUST "TURN BEFORE YOU BURN'!!! IF YOU DON'T TURN YOU WILL BURN IN THE ETERNAL LAKE OF FIRE. JOE IT'S NEVER TOO LATE TO START TELLING THE TRUTH!!! AMEN AND IEN. FROM THE BIG RED MAGA GATOR MAN!!

OD LUCK ROBERT PETERS AND FAMILY.

C'MON MAN!!!!!

TODAY IS 11/19/2021 AND IT IS VERY APPARENT WHY YOUR DEMONIC CONGRESS AND SENATE WOULD NOT LET YOU GET A COGNITIVE EXAM!!! YOU COULD MAYBE CHANGE YOUR NUMBERS IF YOU COULD SPEAK ON ANY SUBJECT FOR 10 MIN.

WITHOUT LOOKING AT YOUR TELEPROMPTER FOR A CANNED SPEECH FROM YOUR HANDLERS!!! YOU ARE

CLAIMING A FANTASTIC JOB IN ALL AREAS OF YOUR JOB!!!! I AM A 100% DISABLED VET AND I HAVE NOT SEEN ANY OF THE EXCESSIVE MONEY TO BUY MORE STUFF THAT YOU ARE BS-ING TO THE PUBLIC. GOD HAS BLESSED THE WORLD WITH MILLIONS OF YEARS OF FOSSIL FUEL! AOC (ABSENCE OF CONSCIENCE) CAN TELL THE WORLD WHEN GREEN NEW GAS WILL PROPEL AIR FORCE 1 AROUND THE WORLD. IT TAKES A TOTAL IMBECILE TO STOP THE OIL SUPPLY FOR 100% OF THIS COUNTRY'S NEEDS PLUS EXPORTS!! AND BEG OUR ENEMIES FOR OIL!!! WHEN IS THE PROPOSED INVENTION OF ENERGY FOR ALL US AIR FORCE JETS NAVY JETS, AIRCRAFT CARRIERS ETC.? I HAVE NOT SEEN ONE ELECTRIC DELTA JET. JOE YOU WOULD HAVE BETTER LUCK TRYING TO COMMUNICATE WITH THE BUILDERS OF UFOS THAT DON'T USE FOSSIL FUEL!!!! I WILL SURVIVE YOUR HELL-BENT TEMPT TO DESTROY THE USA!! YOU ENJOY YOUR COMPLETE TURKEY MEAL AND I'LL ENJOY MY MCDONALD 6 PIECE GET AND SMALL FRENCH FRY DINNER!! BUT DUE TO YOUR GAS BLUNDER, I WILL HAVE TO WALK TO MCDONALDS!

WHILE THE LEADER OF CHINA PUT ON HIS MANLEY DISPLAY OF MANHOOD AND POWER OVER OUR INEPT LEADER WAS HIDING IN HIS MULTI-MILLION DOLLAR BEACH HOUSE BUNKER TRYING TO DEFROST HIS 2 RAISIN-SIZED TESTICLES! IT WAS DURING THE DEEP FREEZE OF 2022&2023 WHILE THE WORLD WAS UNDER AOC GLOBAL WARMING. PRES CHI FLEW HIS SPY BALLOON ACROSS THE US TO SPY ON OUR MAJOR MILITARY INSTALLATIONS! THIS WAS A REAL SHOW OF CHINA'S MANHOOD!!!! SEND BIDEN TO NIKKI MANAZ'S FRIEND'S DOCTOR WHO GAVE HIM A COVID SHOT WHICH RESULTED IN THE SWELLING OF HIS TESTICLES TO THE SIZE OF FULLY RIPENED CALIF. NAVEL ORANGES. IF JOE WENT TO THIS DR. HE MIGHT

GET A BIG RISE FROM SWEETIE PETEY AND HIS BEST FRIEND SAMMY THE LUGGAGE THIEF!!
AND ALL DRAG QUEEN FRIENDS OF CORN-POP-CORN-HOLE JOE!!!!

REPARATIONS FROM HEAVEN: BY THE MAGA
RED GEORGIA GATOR!!!!!
I HAVE BEEN BLESSED BY GOD FOR MANY YEARS TO BE MARRIED TO A BEAUTIFUL, INTELLIGENT BLACK WOMAN WHO IS A 100% DIRECT DESCENDANT OF SLAVE FAMILY IN AMERICA!!!! TODAY SHE HAS FAMILY MEMBERS WHO ARE MILLIONAIRES !!
WE CONDUCTED FAMILY TREE HISTORIES INCLUDING THE USE OF FAMILY DNA! WE DISCOVERED MANY RELATIVES WHO DID NOT MAKE THE BOAT RIDE THEIR DNA WAS FOUND IN SAMPLES OF OVER 100 YR. OLD LION MANURE!! THEY MISSED THE BOAT BUT THE BLESSED ONES WHO MADE THE FREE BOAT RIDE, MANY ARE STILL ALIVE
TODAY=ENJOYING THE BLESSINGS OF REPARATIONS FROM GOD THROUGH WEEKLY PAYCHECKS FROM PERFORMING AN HONEST, FRUITFUL TIME-HONORED TIME KNOWN AS A (JOB)!!!!!! WHEN THE DEMONIC DEMS FALL IN 2024, LIFE WILL TURN TO TRUMP-USA. THANK YOU
US!!!!

JUNE 8 2023
THE BIDEN CRIME FAMILY SAW (GODS)
PROMISE IN ACTION!!! I DON'T BELIEVE BIDEN EVER READ OR BELIEVED THE BIBLE'S WORD OF GOD" IN THE BOOK OF LUKE GOD SPOKE THAT DEEDS AND WORD DONE IN DARKNESS WILL COME TO THE LIGHT AND BE SHOUTED FROM THE ROOFTOPS!! IN JAN 2025 GOD'S CHOSEN VESSEL DONALD J. TRUMP!!!! WILL STAND ON THE ROOF OF THE NOW OUTHOUSE WHITE HOUSE THE SECRETS

OF THE DEEP DARK CORRUPT BIDEN CRIME FAMILY WILL BE SHOUTED TO THE WORLD!! GOD CREATED MAN IN HIS IMAGE NOT IN THE DEMS WOKE IMAGE. GOD MADE ADAM AND EVE--NOT ADAM AND STEVE OR EVE AND JULIE!!! BIDEN LEAVE GOD'S CHILDREN ALONE.

GOD DID NOT CREATE ANY MISTAKES. A BOY IS A BOY AND A GIRL IS A GIRL. ANYTHING ELSE IS THE WORK OF THE DEVIL!! GOD TOLD THE WORLD TO BE FRUITFUL AND MULTIPLY!!

O CORN-HOLED MAN CAN REPRODUCE LIFE!

IS AND DEATH GOD SAID YOU BETTER IN BEFORE YOU BURN!!!! AIDS CAME TO. CALIFORNIA IN THE REAR END OF A

"HUDSON" (ROCK)! THE ONLY THINGS ADAM AND STEVE CAN REPRODUCE ARE MULTIPLE EMPTY TUBES OF "PREP-H" FOR PAINFUL-SWOLLEN "CORN-HOLES'!

TO CONTACT JOE BIDEN ON MATTERS CONCERNING LBGTQ MATTERS CALL HIS

DIRECT LINE 24HRS. A DAY 1-800-69000H(U812)!!

5-10-2023

TODAY DONALD TRUMP APPEARED ON FAKE NEWS TV CNN. IT WAS A WONDERFUL DAY FOR TRUMP! THE DEMONIC LEFT BLEW A FUSE ON NATIONAL NEWS!! INSTEAD OF MAKING TRUMP A FOOL THEY GAVE HIM A NATIONAL PLATFORM!!! RESULTS TRUMP RECEIVED A LARGE BOOST IN HIS POLL!

5-11-23

BRAIN-DEAD BIDEN SOLD OUT THE USA!!!!

GAVE ALL NATIONS FREE ACCESS TO THE US--OPEN BORDERS. FREE FOOD, MEDICINE.INSURANCE, CELL PHONES FREE CLOTHES TO ALL ILLEGAL IMMIGRANTS NO COVID TESTS!!!!5-15-2023

AMERICAN CITIZENS AND DISABLED

AMERICAN VETS WERE PUT OUT OF THEIR HOTEL ROOMS BY NY DEMOCRATS!!!!

THIS WAS DONE BY NEW CITY TO MAKE ROOM FOR ILLEGAL IMMIGRANTS ON 5-16-2023

FBI PROVEN GUILTY IN "H" CLINTON FAKE TRUMP RUSSIA SCAM. OBAMA AND BIDEN WERE ALL WELL INFORMED IN 2016 OF ALL FBI ILLEGAL ACTIONS.

BIDENS AG STOPPED THE HUNTER LAPTOP INVESTIGATION. THE TRUTH GOT TOO HOT FOR THE DEMONIC DEMOCRAT PARTY!

BRAIN DEAD PRES CORN POP PROVED THE OLD SAYING BRAIN-NO PAIN.

DEMOCRATS HAVE NO BRAINS!!!!!

Thanks and accolades to the real author and finisher of this book (JESUS CHRIST) GOD IS PROVING TO THE WORLD THAT EVEN A FRUITFUL TREE CAN GROW FROM A STUMBLING-FUMBLING, bumbling SHAKING in AIR "ROTTEN SEED" LIKE JOE CORN POP BIDEN.

THANK YOU FOR ALL YOUR FREE

INFORMATION. SINCERELY THE MAGA RED FLORIDA GATOR!!!

MY CLOSING STATEMENT

THE STORY NEVER ENDS!! BIDEN'S CLUELESS SENATE INTERVIEWED AN ADULT BIRTHING PERSON AND ASKED IF SHE COULD DESCRIBE A WOMAN AND SHE REPLIED NO! SHE WAS NOT A BIOLOGIST BUT A MOTHER OF TWO!! I THOUGHT A BIOLOGIST STUDIED THINGS UNDER A MICROSCOPE LIKE MICROORGANISMS. IF SHE WAS CONFRONTED WITH A LAWSUIT INVOLVING A HEAD-TO-HEAD COLLISION UNDER THE DESK IN THE OVAL OFFICE BETWEEN BILL AND MONICA, WOULD SHE BE ABLE TO SAY WHO WAS THE GUILTY PARTY? THE EVIDENCE WAS

ON MONICA'S BLUE DRESS!!! WOULD THE NEW JUSTICE CHOKE ON HER ANSWER????
JOE WITH ALL OF HIS MANY YEARS SHOULD KNOW THAT A STRONG OFFENSE IS THE BEST DEFENSE!!!! JOE WITH ALL OF HIS WISDOM OF MILITARY PROCEDURES WAITED UNTIL PUTIN LINED UP 100,000 TROOPS ON THE UKRAINE BORDER. IT TOOK BIMBO TWO WEEKS TO RESPOND. I WON'T MAKE A MOVE UNTIL PUTIN INVADES UKRAINE!! PRESIDENT TRUMP WOULD HAVE PUT A LARGER NUMBER OF MILITARY. TROOPS ON THE UKRAINE BORDER!!!! PUTIN WOULD HAVE TURNED AND RUN BACK HOME!!!!!
JOE DID NOT BELIEVE IN PEACE THROUGH STRENGTH!!!!!! IN 2025 NOBODY F'S WITH THE TRUMPSTER!!!!!

ANOTHER TIME IS HERE TO PUT SUPERMAN BACK IN CHARGE OF THE DEFUNCT
COMMUNIST SOCIALIST MARXIST DEMOCRATS OUT-HOUSE WHITE HOUSE. BARACK PAINTED RED LINES IN THE SAND OF OUR ENEMIES AROUND THE WORLD! THEN HE SAT BACK AND WATCHED THE EMMYS GO AROUND AND BLOW AWAY THE RED LINES ACTION TAKEN BY BARRACK! NO ONE WAS YET AWARE THAT THE ORANGE MAN WAS NOT ONLY THE WORLDS MOST INTELLIGENT LEADER IN HISTORY BUT ALSO THE BEST SURGEON ON EARTH!!!! WHEN ELECTED HE REMOVED THE TESTICLES FROM PUTIN-CHI-PING-IRAN-AND NORTH KOREA!!!
IN AFGHANISTAN TRUMP'S RED LINE WAS BACK OFF OR GET YOUR BEHINDS BLOWN OFF THE MAP!!!! MAKE AMERICA GREAT AGAIN AND ENERGY INDEPENDENT. SELL TO THE WORLD NOT BUY FROM OUR COMMUNIST THIEFS.
UNDER TRUMP 5TH GRADERS READ LIKE 7TH GRADERS. UNDER BIMBO WHO WAS AFRAID TO LET HIS CHILDREN GO TO RACIAL JUNGLE SCHOOLS!! 5TH GRADERS READ

LIKE 3RD GRADERS. WHERE ARE ALL THE BLACK VOTERS IN THIS TRUE STATEMENT!!!! JOE GAVE ALL FOREIGN LEADERS BASKETBALL SIZED TESTICLES. ALL POWER AND ENERGY DURING. GLOBAL WARMING! IN 2022 WE SET RECORD LOW TEMPERATURES AND THE HIGHEST SNOW LEVELS SINCE THE ICE AGE! I PRAYED EVERY WINTER OF 22 THAT (AOC) WOULD OPEN HER GLOBAL WARMING MOUTH. I DID NOT NEED TO GO OUTSIDE AND USE SNOW TO MAKE SNOWBALLS. I JUST WALKED OUTSIDE FOR 3 MOMENTS AND I HAD 2 SNOWBALLS OF MY VERY OWN. OPEN YOUR BIG MOUTH AND BLOW SOME WARM AIR DOWN SOUTH!!!!!!

7-19-2023

FINALLY, THE TRUTH ABOUT THE WEAPONIZATION OF THE DOJ, FBI, AND THE ENTIRE JUSTICE DEPT OF THE USA BY THE BIDEN CRIME FAMILY INC. JOE BIDEN WAS EXPOSED IN THE QUID QUO PRO BY RECEIVING MILLIONS OF DOLLARS FROM UKRAINE BY BRIBING THE UKRAINE LEADER TO FIRE THE PROSECUTOR AGAINST HUNTER BIDEN. BIDEN TOLD THE BOSS IF HE DID NOT FIRE THE PROSECUTOR AGAINST HUNTER IN THE NEXT 6 HOURS. HE WOULD NOT RECEIVE THE BILLION US DOLLARS. BIMBO SAID SON OF A BITCH!!! IN 6 HOURS HE FIRED THE PROSECUTOR!
JOE AND HUNTER RECEIVED 5 MILLION A PIECE!
I ALWAYS WONDERED HOW A SENATOR COULD AFFORD 2 MANSIONS. ONE IN THE BEACH!!
IF JOE WOULD READ HIS BIBLE HE WOULD KNOW IT IS WRITTEN (WORKS, DEEDS, DONE IN DARKNESS WILL COME TO THE LIGHT AND BE SHOUTED FROM THE ROOFTOPS) I BELIEVE THIS WILL BE DONE BY THE PRESIDENT. DONALD TRUMP SHOUTING FROM THE ROOFTOP OF THE OUTHOUSE WHITE HOUSE IN 2025!!!! IT IS MY PERSONAL OPINION AND BELIEF THE ENTIRE

FAMILY AND STAFF OF BIDEN, ESPECIALLY HIS VP, THE QUEEN OF THE WORD SALAD. THAT THEY ALL SUFFER FROM THE SAME MENTAL. THE PROBLEM IS THEIR MENTAL CAPACITY IS INSUFFICIENTLY DEVELOPED BY THEIR
BOMBASTIC KNOWLEDGE OF PHRASEOLOGY!
IN LAYMAN'S TERMS THEY DON'T KNOW WHAT THE HELL THEY ARE TALKING ABOUT!!!! CAN WE GET A BIG JACKASS LAUGH FROM CARMELA!!!

THE INFORMATION CONTAINED IS BASED ON THE BELIEFS AND KNOWLEDGE OF THE WRITER DERIVED FROM SELF-OBTAINED KNOWLEDGE AND INFORMATION FROM CORRECT AND TRUE NEWS
OUTLETS AND STORIES FROM FAKE NEWS
BROADCAST!! I BELIEVE THAT PERSON IN THE WHITE HOUSE IS THE FORERUNNER OF THE ANTICHRIST AND THE PROMOTER OF THE MARK OF THE BEAST!! THE MARK IS THE (D) FOR DEMONIC-DEMOCRAT. WITH THE MARK YOU CAN BUY THE OUT OF THE WORLD CRACK-PIPE PAINTINGS WITHOUT EXPOSING YOUR IDENTITY. I HOPE IF THIS BOOK SELLS FOR LESS THAN $400,000 IN A YEAR, I WILL NOT PAY TAXES LIKE THE "PAINTER". I BELIEVE GOD IS IN CHARGE OF THE CLIMATE NOT RADICAL DEMS!!! I NEARLY FROZE TO DEATH DURING THE GLOBAL WARMING- RETURN OF THE "ICE AGE" 2022-2023 SEASON. IT WAS SAID IF JOE BIDEN WAS IN CHARGE OF THE DESERTS OF THE WORLD, THEY WOULD RUN OUT OF SAND! IF IN CHARGE OF THE OCEANS THERE WOULD BE NO SEA LIFE SINCE JOE WOULD DRAIN THE WATERS OF THE WORLD!!!!! MY PRAYER FOR THE WORLD IS THAT GOD WILL PUT A LEADER BACK IN OFFICE TO (MAKE AMERICA GREAT AGAIN). JOE WHATEVER YOU SAY OR DO IN DARKNESS WILL BE HEARD IN THE LIGHT AND SHOUTED FROM THE ROOFTOPS!!! AMEN!!

RESPECTFULLY THE BIG "RED, WHITE, AND BLUE ATOR!!!!!

FROM THE AUTHOR
THE RED WHITE AND BLUE GATOR
I AM A 76-YEAR-OLD, 100% DISABLED VIETNAM VET AND
RETIRED GOVERNMENT SUPERVISOR. I BELIEVE THE
BEST QUALIFIED FOR ANY JOB SHOULD BE SELECTED
BASED ON POLITICAL BELIEFS!! I HAVE SAID IF I WENT
TO THE CURRENT WHITE HOUSE (OUT-HOUSE) AND SAW
EVERY DEM. POLITICIAN LYING ON THE WHITE HOUSE
LAWN, SCREAMING THEIR BRAINS WERE ON FIRE!!!! I
WOULD NOT TAKE OUT MY FIRE HOSE AND URINATE IN
THEIR EARS TO PUT OUT THE FIRES!!!
(WHY) BRAINS DO NOT BURN AND IT IS A FACT THAT
DEMS DO NOT HAVE ANY BRAINS BETWEEN THEIR
EARS!!!!!
DON'T FIRE THOUSANDS OF ESSENTIAL WORKERS AND
DEPRIVE ALL THE CITIZENS OF THE USA OF ESSENTIAL
PRODUCTS AND NEEDED RESOURCES (GAS-OIL) HEATING
FUEL WHILE IN THE MIDDLE OF 2022-2023 GLOBAL
WARMING BELOW (0) WINTER!!! WELCOME TO THE START
OF THE "BIDEN CABINET MADE INFLATION NATION"
COMPLIMENTS OF CORN HOLE-CORN POP "DRAG QUEEN
KING" BIDEN!

THANKS, AND ACCOLADES TO THE REAL AUTHOR AND
FINISHER OF THIS BOOK {JESUS CHRIST}
GOD IS SHOWING EVEN A
A PRODUCTIVE TREE CAN GROW FROM A STUMBLING
FUMBLING
HAND SHAKING NO ONE IN MID-AIR. "ROTTEN -SEED!!!!
"JOE CORN POP BIDEN"
THANKS, FROM THE RED GATOR!!!!!
THIS BOOK IS ALL ABOUT "YOU"!!!

YOUR ADMINISTRATION IS MORE POWERFUL THAN 1,000 TRAIN WRECKS!!!!! YOU DOG-FACED PONY-SOLDIER!!!!!

MEN BEWARE!!!!!
ANY MAN PLANNING TO VISIT THE CNN-FAKE NEWS HEADQUARTERS IN ATLANTA GA. BE SURE TO PURCHASE AND WEAR A HIGHLY SENSITIVE ENHANCED HEARING DEVICE TO AVOID ANY SUDDEN CONTACT FROM "BEHIND" WITH [DON-ANDERSON THE TUBE MAN BEHIND THE DESK ALL OF WHOM MAY BE WEARING SNEAKERS!!!!!

!EXTRA-EXTRA! READ ALL ABOUT IT.
WHEN ALL DEMONIC
DEMOCRATS WERE IN THE WOMB, GOD WAS GIVING YOU PHYSICAL PROPERTIES-
"BRAINS" THE DEMS ALL RAN FOR COVER! THEY THOUGHT GOD SAID RAINS AND DID NOT WANT ANY!!!

FAA NORTHERN TRIANGLE ALERT!!!!
STRANGE LOOKING BORDER
CZAR PATROLLING 60,000
MIGRANTS HEADING TOWARDS THE USA! CZAR VP SEEN FLYING ON A GREEN NEW GAS-POWERED BROOM!!!
LOTS OF HORSES LAUGHING BUT
NO SOLUTIONS OFFERED.
IT'S A BIRD-IT'S A PLANE-NO
IT'S A FLYING HORSE
LAUGHING VP---GO CAMEL-AI

WHEN YOU ARE A 17-YEAR-OLD WHITE MALE AND YOUR FATHER'S HOME HOMETOWN IS BURNED TO THE GROUND BY HATE GROUPS AND BLM RIOTERS AND YOU COME TO TOWN TO HELP PROTECT PRIVATE PROPERTY, DO MINOR FIRST AID, AND HELP PUT OUT FIRES. THEN

YOU GET IN DEADLY TROUBLE WITH RIOTERS AND IN SELF-DEFENSE KILL 2 PEOPLE AND WOUND 1. THEN THE PRESIDENT GOES ON NATL. TV AND CALLS YOU A WHITE SUPREMACIST. GUILTY-GUILTY. THIS FOR THE TIME BEING IS THE LAND WHERE YOU ARE INNOCENT UNTIL PROVEN GUILTY BY A GROUP OF YOUR PEERS. WHAT SAY YOU JOE!! DID YOU TURN THE COUNTRY OVER TO YOUR FRIEND (PUTIN)? DON'T FORGET XI! THIS IS STILL FOR THE TIME BEING THE "USA" NOT THE USSR C'MON MAN!!!!!

JOE BIDEN WILL BE FOREVER REMEMBERED AS THE MOST INEPT PERFORMING, CLUELESS, SLEEPY, GAS-FILLED LEADER IN THE ENTIRE WORLD!!!!
C-MON MAN!! YOU WERE FREE TO THE WORLD WITH (YOUR) GAS!!!
WHAT ABOUT YOURS, IT'S THE HIGHEST IN HISTORY DUE ONLY TO YOUR BROKEN POLICIES!!!!
C; MON MAN !!!!!!!!!!!!!!!!!!!!!!

I HAVE BEEN TOLD THAT I HATE TOO MANY PEOPLE. THE TRUTH IS THE ONLY PEOPLE I HAVE NO RESPECT FOR ARE ALL OF THE RADICAL DEMONIC DEMOCRATIC PARTY!!! ESPECIALLY THE CONSTANT CHEATING, LYING BETTER THAN ANYONE ELSE RULES FOR ME NOT FOR THE CHAIRWOMAN, BIMBO BIDEN, HORSE-LAUGHING CAMEL-AH HARRIS WHO WAS CREATING HAVOC IN HER CALIF. POSITION MADE NATL. NEWS FOR HER GIANT LAWSUIT AGAINST A LARGE MORTGAGE COMPANY IN MICH. FOR REPOSSESSING HOMES FOR ALMOST NO REASON! AT THAT TIME I HAD MADE A LATE A LATE PAYMENT ON MY HOUSE BUT WAS UNAWARE OF A $39.00 LATE FEE. I RECEIVED A FORECLOSURE NOTICE AND I HAD

2 WEEKS TO VACATE! I HIRED A LAWYER AND QUALIFIED FOR A $40,000 FREE LOAN TO GIVE TO THE MORTGAGE COMPANY.

THEY REFUSED!!! I CONTACTED CAMELAS OFFICE AND ASKED FOR HELP---THEY REFUSED HELP AND SAID GOOD LUCK!!! THE SHERIFF CAME BY WITH 6 OFFICERS AND SAID I HAD 5 DAYS TO GET OUT!!!! NO PROBLEM- WE WERE GONE IN 4 DAYS TO FLORIDA. THE STATE OF NATIONAL FREEDOM RICK SCOTT.

TODAY IF I WAS WALKING DOWN PENN. AVE AND I CAME UPON BIDEN.CAMELA, ADAM, BERNIE, NANCY, JERRY, AND CHUCK WERE ALL ON THE GROUND YELLING HELP OUR BRAINS ARE ON FIRE!!! I WOULD NOT PULL OUT MY PRIVATE HOSE AND URINATE IN THEIR EARS TO PUT OUT THE FIRES!!!!

HEY JOEY BABY!

I HAVE HEARD THAT YOUR RADICAL MARXIST SOCIALIST PARTY MEMBERS SAY ON NATIONAL TV THEY DON'T HAVE A MAGIC WAND TO STOP THE HIGH GAS PRICES!!!! BUT SHE WAS ABLE TO GIVE A BIG VP HORSE LAUGH !! KUDOS

PLEASE LET MY 9-YEAR-OLD GRANDSON GIVE YOU A FANTASTIC SOLUTION TO THE PROBLEM!!!! SIMPLY PULL YOUR HEAD OUT OF YOUR REAR END AND RECIND EVERY EX. ORDER YOU CANCELED FROM THE GREATEST PRESIDENT EVER. THE TRUMPSTER!!!!

C'MON MAN GET WITH THE PROGRAM!!!!

SOUND THE HEAVENLY ALARM!!!!
BIDEN AND HIS DEMONIC BAND OF RADICAL IDIOTS HAVE FINALLY
GONE BEYOND STUPIDITY!!!
ONLY GOD HIMSELF AND DONALD
TRUMP CAN SAVE THIS COUNTRY!!!!!!

ON DEC 10 2021 CAMELA CAST THE NEEDED VOTE TO
PUT A RACIST DEMONIC FEMALE DISTRICT ATTORNEY IN
OFFICE IN BOSTON MASS. THIS TOTAL IDIOT PUT UP A LIST
OF FELONY CRIMES THAT SHE WOULD NOT PROSECUTE.
JAIL IS NOT NEEDED BY HER UNDERSTANDING. SHE IS
JUST ANOTHER GEORGE SOROS-APPOINTED DISASTER!!!
WHO IN AMERICA WOULD LOVE TO HAVE A LOVED ONE
MURDERED AND THE CRIMINAL WAS TOLD IT'S OK, GO
HOME AND COME BACK WHENEVER YOU WANT. JAIL
WOULD BE TOO HARD FOR YOU BABY! THE BORDER IS
TOTALLY OUT OF CONTROL AND BOZO BIDEN APPOINTS
ANOTHER JERK TO BE THE BORDER COM. WHO HATE
THE BORDER GUARDS, POLICE, AND LAW OFFICIALS.
WITH VACCINE SHOTS FOR YOU AND FOR ME!!! ILLEGAL
IMMIGRANTS CAN BRING IN ANY AND ALL ILLNESS OR
LETHAL DRUGS AND GET PAID $450.000 BECAUSE YOU
BROKE THE USA LAWS.
THOUSANDS OF AMERICANS ARE BARELY MAKING IT
DUE TO BIDEN INFLATION AND PAYING AMERICANS TO
STAY HOME AND THE TAXPAYERS WILL GIVE YOU FREE
MONEY!!!!!! NOW NOT TO BE OUTDONE BOZO BIDEN
WANTS TO DRAFT WOMEN 19-21 YRS. OLD INTO THE
MILITARY, IT IS THE MEN'S TO PROTECT OUR NATION
AGAINST ALL ENEMIES BOTH FOREIGN AND DOMESTIC!!!!!
BIDEN CANNOT!!!!! WOMEN CAN ENLIST AND DO A
WONDERFUL JOB AT WHATEVER THEY CHOOSE TO DO!!!!
LOOTING IS ACCEPTED SINCE THESE POOR CITIZENS DO
NOT HAVE A JOB (THANKS TO BIDEN) AND THEY ARE
HUNGRY AND MUST EAT DIAMONDS AND FURS AND
$1500.00 PURSES. I COULD AGREE THEY STOLE FRUIT AND
BREAD OR OTHER EDIBLE ITEMS. WHEN I WAS 10 YRS,
IF I STOLE A 5-CENT PIECE OF BUBBLEGUM YOU WENT
TO JUVENILE COURT!!!! IF GOD AND TRUMP DON'T GET
BACK SOON THERE MAY NOT BE A WORLD- MUCH LESS
THE USA! OR THE DEMONIC LEFTS UNITED SOCIALIST

STATES OF CHINA-RUSSIA-NORTH KOREA!!!!! GIVE JOE A BRAIN SCAN TO SEE IF ANYBODY'S HOME!!!!!!!
MA 100% DISABLED VIETNAM VET LIVING ON A LIMITED INCOME WAS TOO WEAK TO GO R THIS COUNTRY BUT HE WANTS TO SEND WOMEN AND NOT HELP THE VETS!!!!! BUILD YOUR OWN BEACH BUNKER BASEMENT=DITCH YOUR TELEPROMPTER SINCE YOU CAN'T READ!!! SINCERELY FROM THE (GATORMAN!!!!!!!)

SEPTEMBER 2023
A WARNING AND INDICTMENT OF AND TO THE NON-BELIEVERS OF THE TRUE BOOK OF LAW "THE HOLY BIBLE" THE RADICAL MEMBERS OF THE DEMONIC DEMOCRATIC PARTY! THIS INCLUDES THE #1 CRIME SYNDICATE BIDEN FAMILY, MENDEZ FAMILY, AND THE ENTIRE BIDEN GOVERNMENT IN THE OUT HOUSE - WHITE HOUSE, CONGRESS, SENATE, FBI, DOJ ALL RADICAL LEFT DEMOCRATIC, SOCIALIST, MARXIST FOLLOWERS!!! FROM THE WORD OF GOD
"JAMES CHAPTER 5 1-7. GO NOW, YE RICH MEN, WEEP AND HOWL FOR YOUR MISERIES THAT SHALL COME UPON YOU. YOUR RICHES ARE CORRUPTED AND YOUR GARMENTS ARE MOTH EATEN. YOUR GOLD AND SILVER IS CANKERED AND THE RUST OF THEM SHALL BE WITNESS AGAINST YOU AND SHALL YOUR FLESH AS IT WERE FIRE. YOU HAVE HEAPED TREASURE TOGETHER FOR THE LAST DAYS. I HAVE LIVED IN PLEASURE ON THE HAND BEEN WANTON. YOU HAVE NOURISHED YOUR HEARTS, AS IN, A DAY OF SLAUGHTER. DEMS REMEMBER GOD MADE MAN AND WOMAN (ADAM AND EVE) NOT ADAM AND STEVE!! PLEASE NO MORE WHITE HOUSE DRAG QUEEN PARTIES FOR YOUR ADMINISTRATION !!!!
MY ADVICE TO ALL PEOPLE WHO SUPPORT THE DEMONIC (D) PARTY-{YOU BETTER TURN BEFORE YOU BURN} GOD SAID NO!! SIN IS GOING TO ENTER IN!!!!! YOU BETTER

TURN BEFORE YOU BURN IN THE ETERNAL LAKE OF FIRE!!!! AMEN&AMEN.

WHO IS THE REAL JOE B.?? AKA ROBERT PETERS-AKA ROBERT WARE OR JRB WARE? WILL THE REAL BIMBO BIDEN PLEASE STAND UP!!!! JOE BIDEN IS THE REAL BIG GUY, HEAD OF THE BIDEN {RICO) CRIME SYNDICATE FAMILY!!! JOE YOU LAUGH WHEN SOMEONE SAYS (WHERE'S THE MONEY HOW ABOUT OVER 100 BANK INQUIRIES NOT VERIFIED? HOW MANY OFF-SHORE BANK ACCOUNTS DO YOU HAVE? A WORD TO THE WISE JOEY BABY!! IT IS ALWAYS BETTER TO KEEP YOUR MOUTH CLOSED AND LET PEOPLE THINK YOU ARE STUPID. DON'T OPEN YOUR MOUTH WIDE AND PROVE YOU ARE!!! EVERY DAY ANOTHER LAYER OF THE BIDEN "RICO" SYNDICATE FAMILY ONION IS BEING PEELED AWAY! ELECTION INTERFERENCE BY TRUMP "MY ASS" I HAVE VIDEO RECORDINGS OF STACY ABRAHAMS CONFRONTING GOV. KEMP SHOUTING HE RIGGED THE ELECTIONS!!!! RICO FOR REPUBLICANS, BUT NOT FOR DEMONIC DEMOCRATS!!! BIMBO YOU HAVE SINGLE-HANDEDLY TOTALLY CORRUPTED THE DEPT OF JUSTICE FBI AND DESTROYED THE ENTIRE US ECONOMY WITH BIDEN-DEMONICS!! RUINED THE #1 MILITARY IN THE WORLD!! DESTROYED THE EDUCATION SYSTEM FOR ALL AMERICAN CHILDREN!!! DESTROYED THE TRANSPORTATION IN LAND SEA AND AIR WITH CORN HOLE PETE!
AIN'T EVEN FIX A POTHOLE!!!! IS IT STRANGE. EVERY CASE OF RICO IS BY RADICAL DEM
BILLIONAIRE GEORGE SOROS PAID TO HAVE ALL DUMB-ASSED DAS BEG TO PROSECUTE YOUR ONLY REP CHALLENGER!!
WHEN IS YOUR NEXT SCHEDULED DRAG QUEEN PARTY AT THE NOW OUT-HOUSE WHITE-HOUSE?

BE SURE TO INVITE ALL OF YOUR SWEETIE HAPPY
CABINET DRESSED IN BEAUTIFUL PINK DRESSES AND
SPANDEX!!!! JUST WHAT AMERICAN CHILDREN NEED TO
SEE!!!! OPEN THE GATES OF (HELL)!! TRY INVITING ADAM
AND EVE- NOT PETIE AND SAMMY!!!

GOD BLESS THE USA IN 2025-"MAKE AMERICA GREAT
AGAIN!!!!" WHAT ABOUT YOUR SOUTHERN BORDER AND
YOUR BRAINLESS 2-BORDER CZARS!! OVER 5 MILLION
ILLEGAL CRIMINALS AND DRUG DEALERS WALKING
INTO AMERICA WITH A JOE BIDEN CELL PHONE!!!!! DON'T
FORGET YOUR DAY LATE-DOLLAR SHORT VACATION TO
HAWAII.

WHAT A POWERFUL OFFER!!!! $700.00 TO ALL FAMILIES
THAT LOST EVERYTHING INCLUDING FAMILY MEMBERS!!!!
WHAT A WORTHLESS DISPLAY OF SYMPATHY!! I BET YOU
MOVED THE CROWD WHEN YOU SAID YOU ALMOST LOST
OUR CORVETTE IN A FIRE THAT NEVER REACHED UR
HOUSE!! DID YOUR RESPONSE TEAM DERS ENJOY THEIR
NIGHTS IN $1200.A NIGH EL ROOMS?? JOE DID YOU FIND
ANY YOUNG.

GIRLS THAT DID NOT HAVE THEIR HAIR BURNT OFF!! IF
YOU EVER TRIED TO SMELL MY GRANDDAUGHTER'S HAIR
YOUR NOSE WOULD BE IN THE BACK OF YOUR HEAD!!!!!
START PAYING AMERICAN CITIZENS MONEY FOR FOOD,
CLOTHING, HOUSING AND MEDICINE. QUIT PAYING
CHINA FOR ALL ILLEGAL DRUGS!

FINALLY FOR YOU JOE! THERE WAS A TIME IN MY LIFE
WHEN I HAD ONE FOOT ON A BANANA PEEL AND ONE
FOOT IN THE GRAVE!!!!

MY WIFE MADE ME TURN TO GOD!!! ONE NIGHT ABOUT
2:00 AM 1 WAS READING MY BIBLE AND I HEARD A VERY
LOUD VOICE TELLING ME TO STOP READING AND LISTEN!
I ASKED MY WIFE IF SHE HEARD THE VOICE AND SHE
REPLIED NO. I JUST SAT STILL FOR A WHILE THEN PICKED

UP MY BIBLE AND BEGAN READING AGAIN. SUDDENLY THE VOICE RETURNED LOUDER THAN BEFORE AND SAID THE END IS NEAR AND IT'S TIME FOR EVERYONE TO EXAMINE THEIR LIFE AND LIFESTYLES AND IF THE LIVES THEY WERE LIVING WERE NOT PLEASING IN THE SIGHT OF GOD!! AND IF YOU WANT TO GO TO HEAVEN ONE DAY YOU MUST "TURN BEFORE YOU BURN"!!! IF YOU DON'T TURN YOU WILL BURN IN THE ETERNAL LAKE OF FIRE. JOE IT'S NEVER TOO LATE TO START TELLING THE TRUTH!!! AMEN AND AMEN. FROM THE BIG RED MAGA GATOR MAN!!

GOOD LUCK ROBERT PETERS AND FAMILY.

JOE, PLEASE GIVE US BACK OUR NATURAL GAS AND OIL TO KEEP US WARM I HAVE BURNED THE LAST OF MY FURNITURE TO KEEP THE KIDS WARM DURING THIS GLOBAL WARMING BY AOC.

RISE O'KEEPER OF THE SUNSHINE, RUSH TO OUR RESCUE O-GREAT KEEPER OF THE ATMOSPHERE! WHERE ARE YOU HIDING THE O-GREAT WORLD THERMOSTAT? YES, YOU OH KEEPER OF THE WORLD HEAT!!!

AOC APPEARS BEFORE WE ALL FREEZE TO DEATH IN THIS HUGE WINTER STORM. 12 INCHES OF SNOW IN NEW YORK CITY!!!!! THE CITIZENS OF NEW YORK ARE BRACING FOR MAYBE 2 FEET OF FROZEN HEAT!!!!

SUPPLY THEM WITH HEATING OIL TO KEEP WARM AND COOK HOT MEALS!!

THE BIDENS HAVE A SECRET IN TIMES LIKE THESE TO KEEP HOT!! WHEN A COLD FORECAST ARRIVES THE ENTIRE BIDEN FAMILY INC. GO TO THEIR FAVORITE SUPER HOT MEXICAN RESTAURANT AND ORDER THE HOTTEST, SPICY FOOD AND EAT UP THEIR FILL! THEN THEY USE THEIR SECRET. THEY ALL EAT A GREAT HELPING OF ICE CREAM FOR DESSERT AND FOR A FIRE EXTINGUISHER. WHEN THEIR BOWELS START TO RUMBLE THEY ALL RUN

TO THEIR THRONES AND SCREAM "COME ON ICE CREAM",
SPEAK OH LIPS OF FIRE, OH TOOTHLESS WONDER. COME
ON ICE CREAM AND COOL THE FLAMES!

JOE CONTINUE TO TAKE YOUR GAS TO FRANCE AND
DROP IT ON THE WORLD STAGE!!!!! THE PYTHONS IN
MIAMI WILL BE FALLING FROM THE TREES AGAIN, NOT
SINCE OBAMA WAS IN CHARGE!!!!

SOUND THE HEAVENLY ALARMI!! BIDEN AND HIS
DEMONIC BAND OF RADICAL IDIOTS HAVE FINALLY
GONE BEYOND STUPIDITY!!! ONLY GOD HIMSELF AND
DONALD TRUMP CAN SAVE THIS COUNTRY!!!!!!

ON DEC 10 2021 CAMELA CAST THE NEEDED VOTE TO PUT
A DEMONIC LEFT-RACIST FEMALE DISTRICT ATTORNEY
IN OFFICE IN BOSTON MASS.

THIS TOTAL IDIOT PUT UP A LIST OF FELONY CRIMES SHE
WOULD NOT PROSECUTE. JAIL IS NOT NEEDED BY HER
UNDERSTANDING. SHE IS JUST ANOTHER GEORGE SOROS-
FUNDED DISASTER! WHO IN AMERICA WOULD LOVE TO
HAVE A LOVED ONE MURDERED AND THE CRIMINAL
WAS TOLD BY THE JUDGE TO GO HOME AND COME BACK
WHEN IT IS OK BY YOU!!! JAIL MIGHT BE TOO HARD FOR
YOU "BABY". THE BORDER IS TOTALLY OUT OF CONTROL
AND BOZO BIDEN APPOINTS ANOTHER CLUELESS BORDER
COMMANDER WHO HATED THE BORDER GUARDS AND
THE POLICE AND LAW OFFICIALS WITH VACCINE SHOTS
FOR YOU BUT NOT FOR ME!!! ILLEGAL IMMIGRANTS CAN
BRING IN ANY AND ALL ILLEGAL DRUGS, OR SICKNESS
AND GET PAID $450,000 BECAUSE THEY CANNOT FIND
MYSTERY CHILDREN THEY COULD NOT PROVE WERE
THEIRS. THOUSANDS OF AMERICANS RARELY, MAKE IT
DUE TO BIDEN INFLATION AND PAYING MILLIONS OF
AMERICANS OF AMERICANS TO STAY HOME WITH EXTRA
PAY!

THEIR MONEY IS BEING PAID BY THE FAITHFUL AMERICANS WHO ARE STILL WORKING. BIDEN LOVES THE TAX-PAYERS, JUST PAY YOURS AND JOE'S FAIR SHARE!!! NOW SINCE YOUNG AMERICANS ARE JOINING THE MILITARY LIKE BEFORE BIMBO SAID HE WANTS TO DRAFT WOMEN BETWEEN THE AGES OF 19 AND 21.

BIMBO, IT IS THE MEN OF AMERICAS JOB TO PROTECT OUR NATION FROM ALL ENEMIES BOTH FOREIGN AND DOMESTIC. I VOLUNTEERED FOR MY COUNTRY! JOE DID YOU EVER SERVE EXCEPT MAYBE THE CUB SCOUTS !!!! LOOTING IS NOW LEGAL FOR GOODS UP TO $950.00 SINCE THEY ARE NOT WORKING AND MUST EAT DIAMONDS, FUR COATS AND $1500.00 PURSES!!! | COULD AGREE IF THEY WERE STEALING EDIBLE ITEMS. WHEN I WAS 10 YEARS OLD AND STOLE A 5-CENT PIECE OF BUBBLE GUM AND GOT CAUGHT YOU WENT TO JUVENILE COURT!! IF OD AND TRUMP DON'T GET BACK SOON THERE MAY NOT BE A USA!! IT WILL BE THE UNITED SOCIALIST LEFTIST MARXIST STATES OF CHINA, RUSSIA, AND NORTH REA!!!!!! GIVE BIDEN A BRAIN SCAN TO SEE IF ANYBODY'S HOME!!!! I AM A

6 DISABLED VIETNAM VET AND I DON'T STEAL TO SURVIVE!!! BRAVE VETS KNOW HOW TO SURVIVE!!!!! BRAVE VET V HOW TO SURVIVE !!!!! WE ARE SMELLY WALMART SHOPPERS!!!!

JOE YOU WILL BE THE KING OF ALL USA CRIMINALS IF YOU CANCEL GUN SALES TO THE PUBLIC AND GUARANTEE THAT THUG. DEMOCRAT POLITICIANS WILL HAVE HIGH-PAID ARMED GUARDS AND ALL CROOKS WILL REMAIN ARMED!!!!!! LET ALL DEMONIC MALE CHILDREN MARRY ONLY TRANS MEN!!! NO LONGER WILL WE NEED ROE V WADE!!!!! AS FOR SCHOOL LOANS, I THINK THE GOVERNMENT SHOULD CREATE A 10% ADDITIONAL INCOME TAX FOR ALL COLLEGE GRADS. TAX WILL BE IN

EFFECT UNTIL DEATH OR THE LOAN PAID OFF. I PAID MY LOAN IN FULL BY SERVING
4 YRS. ON THE FIRING LINE IN N. VIET NAM. AT 1 AM NOW A 100% DISABLED VET DUE TO PTSD CAUSED BY HAVING TO KILL TWO WELL-DRESSED MEN IN BLACK SILK PAJAMAS WITH MY BARE HANDS!!!! I WOULD FIGHT FOR THIS COUNTRY AGAIN AS SOON AS A PRESIDENT WHO IS SMART. STRONG AND INTELLIGENT TAKE CHARGE OF THIS RAPIDLY DETERIORATING COUNTRY!!!!!! A IRON MAN --NOT A CORN POP!!!!!
DONALD TRUMP IN 2024!!!! GIVE SLEEPY JOE THE MENTAL ACUITY EXAM AND SEE IF JOE CAN TELL HIS WIFE FROM HIS SISTER!!!!!!! WHAT ABOUT THE 5 MILLION ON YOUR IRS FORM? PAY YOUR FAIR SHARE BIMBO!!!!!
PAUL P. WILL PAY YOUR BILL FOR YOU !!!!!!

THE ENTIRE CAST OF THE WIZARD OF OZ IS REUNITED AND ALIVE IN OUR NATION'S WHITE HOUSE!!!!! OUR LEADERS CAN HARDEN OUR SCHOOLS BUT THE WICKED WITCH WHO RODE OVER THE NORTHERN TRIANGLE ON A BRAND-NEW AOC DESIGNED GREEN NEW GAS POWERED BROOM LEFT A LARGE GREEN GAS VAPOR TRAIL OVER THE SOUTHERN TRIANGLE!!!!! ANNOUNCED TODAY HER BRILLIANT IDEA TO PAY BILLIONS TO THE ALREADY BILLIONAIRE LEADERS TO FIND A WAY TO KEEP THE THOUSANDS OF ILLEGAL IMMIGRANTS IN THEIR OWN COUNTRY!!!! THE SCARECROW (IF I ONLY HAD A BRAIN-I'D BE DANGEROUS-LEADER HAIR SNIFFING ALWAYS ON VACATION PRESIDENT) WOULD FIGURE OUT HOW TO LISTEN TO HIS MILITARY LEADERS WE WOULD NOT HAVE ARMED THE TALIBAN WITH MORE WEAPONS THAN THE USA CRIMINALS !!!!! THEY CRIED "THANK YOU CORN POP" THE US PAYS MORE MONEY THAN ANYONE TO WORLD ORGANIZATIONS AND TODAY THEY ANNOUNCED THEY WOULD SEND CASH CARDS AND PROVIDE LEGAL ADVICE

TO SCAM THEIR WAY TO LEGAL ENTRY!!!!! THE TIN MAN -IF I ONLY HAD A HEART GARLAND, WOULD EXAMINE THE HEARTS OF THE GEORGE SOROS APPOINTED NO-TIME FOR CRIME RUN OVER ME AND MY BABY AND GO FREE RADICAL DEMONIC LEFT DA'S IN THE DEMONIC RUN STATES! MY ADVICE TO ALL DEMOCRATS RUNNING FOR REELECTION SHOULD BEND OVER- PUT YOUR EMPTY HEADS BETWEEN YOUR LEGS AND KISS YOUR BRAINLESS BEHINDS GOODBYE!!!! FINAL WORD FOR THE SCARECROW---BESIDE A BRAIN- GROW A PAIR OF TESTICLES!!!!! NOW ALL DEMONCRATES CLICK YOUR RUBY SLIPPERS TOGETHER AND GO HOME!!!!! I WAS ONCE VERY PROUD TO BE A 100% DISABLED VIETNAM VET IN THE USA I AM ASHAMED TO THINK 4YRS OF HELL ARE NOW IN VAIN!!!! GOD PLEASE PUT THE CHILDREN OUTPUT THE ADULT REPUBLICANS BACK IN CHARGE. STOP DRILLING FOR GREEN NEW GAS!!!!!!!!

WELCOME BACK TO REALITY!!!16-5-22.
I JUST WITNESSED A REMARKABLE WORLD LEADER SHOW THE WORLD HOW A LEADER WITH A WORKING BRAIN CAN LEAD A SAFE, POWERFUL, TRUTHFUL NATION WITHOUT A SINGLE IGNORANT GAFF!! I REMEMBER A SAYING IN MY CHILDHOOD "JUST LET PEOPLE THINK YOU ARE BRAINLESS- DON'T OPEN THAT HAIR-SMELLING HOLE IN YOUR FACE AND (PROVE IT OUT LOUD)!!!! JOE COULD DRAW A CROWD LIKE THAT IF HE WOULD ONLY GO BACK TO DAY 1 IN OFFICE AND RECIND EVERY ECONOMY KILLING ORDER HE PUT IN PLACE AT THE CLUELESS REQUEST OF HIS CLUELESS MARKIST, COMMUNIST, RADICAL ISLAMIC DEMOCRATIC SWIMMING POOL FULL OF DEPLORABLES. I GUESS I WILL NEVER KNOW HOW LAZY CRIMINAL SMASH-AND-GRAB BODIES CAN SWALLOW AND PROCESS AND PASS ROLEX WATCHES, DESIGNER HANDBAGS AND OTHER INANIMATE OBJECTS

!!!! I GUESS IF THE DEMOCRATS BELIEVE MEN CAN GET PREGNANT AND GIVE BIRTH THROUGH REAR-END BIRTH CANALS!!! WE STILL HAVE NO IDEA WHO GAVE BIRTH TO OUR TRANSPORTATION LEADERLESS HEAD. I PRAY THEY HAVE A LARGE SUPPLY OF PREP!!!! I KNOW OUR NEW SUPREME COURT JUSTICE CANNOT ANSWER WHAT A WOMAN IS!!!!

THE GREATEST FINANCIAL INCREASE CAME IN 2021-2022 THANKS TO CORN POP CLUELESS BIDEN!
THE PHARMACEUTICAL BUSINESS
INCLUDING THE FAKE COVID-19 GET THE SHOT AND NO COVID-19 REGARDLESS OF AGE LIE. AND THE TREMENDOUS INCREASE IN THE SALE OF PREP-H AFTER BIMBOS OUT-HOUSE WHITE HOUSE DRAG QUEEN CORN-HOLDERS LBGTQ CONVENTION. THE FOLLOWING DAY THE NATIONAL SALES OF PREP-H FOR THE RELIEF OF TOOTHLESS WONDER AND LIPS OF FIRE BURNING RECEIVERS PAIN!!!!!
ALSO THE INCREASED SALES OF KY-8
FOR THE YOUNG & TENDER NEW CORN-HOLERS. THIS IS A GREAT WASTE OF MILLIONS OF DOLLARS GOING DOWN THE WHITE HOUSE CONSTANTLY, ENLARGING THE WHITE HOUSE CORN- HOLE. THANK YOU, CORN-HOLE, CORN POP BIDEN.

12-22-2022
THE FAR LEFT DEMONIC, RADICAL MARXIST DEMOCRAT BRAIN DEAD LEADER STRIKES A DEATH BLOW TO ARIZONA RESIDENTS!!! ARIZONA DOES NOT HAVE A NATURAL BORDER LIKE TEXAS, SO ARIZONA'S GOV. BUILT A WALL USING EMPTY RAIL CARS TO HELP SLOW THE ILLEGAL MIGRANTS, DRUGS, CHILD MOLESTERS AND MURDER SUSPECTS INTO THE CITIES AND FAMILIES OF

FREE AMERICANS. ALL AMERICANS NOW CONSIDERED 2ND. RATE CITIZENS.!!!!

HEY JOE! QUIT PAYING PEOPLE TO NOT WORK AND REDUCE THE NEED FOR ILLEGAL WORKERS!!!! HUNTER BIDEN'S FRIENDS IN CHINA PAID FOR JOE'S GREAT WALL AROUND HIS BEACH HOUSE BUNKER!! A WALL FOR ME BUT NONE FOR THEE!!!! JOE REMOVED THE ARIZONA WALL!!! SAYING UP YOUR CORNHOLE ARIZONA!!!!!! AND NO!!! PREP-H!!!! HAIL TO THE NEW MASTER OF LBGTO CEREMONIES WHO PUT ON A NATIONAL TV SODOM AND GOMORRAH DRAG QUEEN SHOW ON NATIONAL TV!! THE SHOW WAS PUT ON FOR JOE'S NEW WAVE CABINET WHICH INCLUDES MR & MR, MRS PETE, AND THEIR BEHIND BEST FRIEND SAMMY THE LUGGAGE THIEF AND NUCLEAR WASTE EXPERT. THIS FANTASTIC DISGUSTING SHOW HAD MY CHILDREN WANTING TO KNOW IF IT WAS OK FOR BOYS TO DRESS UP LIKE WOMEN!!!! I TOLD THEM GOD SAID THIS WAS DEFINITELY AGAINST THE WORD OF GOD!!! SOUNDS LIKE THE SECOND COMING OF SODOM AND GOMORRAH TO THE ONCE GOD-BASED USA (SAD)!!

THE ANTICHRIST HAS ARRIVED AND IS HARD AT WORK!!! IF YOU DO NOT HAVE THE "MARK OF THE BEAST COVID-19 VACCINE" YOU CANNOT EAT INDOORS, FLY ON A PLANE GO TO THE MOVIES, OR HOLD A JOB TO SUPPORT YOUR FAMILY. THE ANTICHRIST JOE BIMBO BIDEN AND HIS ARMY THE SOCIALIST DEMONIC DEMONCRATE PARTY SAID ONCE ILLEGAL IMMIGRANTS ARE IN THE USA THAT ICE WILL NOT BE ABLE TO LOCATE THEM FOR DEPORTATION. "BULL'S-IT" BILLIONAIRES HAVE MICROCHIPS INJECTED INTO THEIR CHILDREN AND PETS IN CASE A CROOK WANTS RANSOM FOR THEIR RETURN!!! INSERT A CHIP INCLUDING THE COVID-19 VACCINE IN ALL ILLEGAL IMMIGRANTS OVER 10YRS, OLD. THIS WOULD ALSO BE A GREAT POLICY FOR ALL RADICAL LEFT DAS WHEN

LETTING DANGEROUS CRIMINALS OUT EARLY, YOU CAN RUN BUT YOU CAN'T HIDE!!!!
THE BIBLE SAYS WHAT'S DONE IN DARKNESS WILL COME TO THE LIGHT AND BE SHOUTED FROM THE ROOFTOP!!!
NO SHOT JOB PER ANTICHRIST JOE BIDEN.
AMEN AND AMEN

EXTRA-EXTRA! READ ALL ABOUT IT.
WHEN ALL DEMONIC
DEMOCRATS WERE IN THE WOMB, GOD WAS GIVING OUT PHYSICAL PROPERTIES-
"BRAINS" THE DEMS ALL RAN FOR COVER! THEY THOUGHT GOD SAID RAINS AND DID NOT GET ANY!!!!!!

JOE BIDEN'S RULES FOR CHESS!
THE FIRST MOVE IS TO PLACE YOUR KING IN THE MIDDLE OF THE FRONT LINE!!! SECOND MOVE CHECKMATE BOZO!!!! HOW CAN YOU TELL
WHEN A DEMOCRAT
IS TELLING A LIE!!!!!
THEIR LIPS ARE MOVING!!!!!

12-22-2022
THE FAR-LEFT DEMONIC, RADICAL, MARXIST, DEMOCRAT, BRAIN DEAD LEADER STRIKES A DEATH BLOW TO ARIZONA RESIDENTS!!! ARIZONA DOES NOT HAVE A GOD MADE NATURAL BORDER LIKE TEXAS ARIZONA'S GOV. BUILT A WALL WITH RAIL CARS ON TOP OF THE GROUND TO HELP DETER THE ILLEGAL PEOPLE OVER-RUNNING THE STATE! ALSO SLOW THE FLOW OF ILLEGAL DRUGS, CHILD MOLESTERS AND MURDER SUSPECTS INTO THE CITIES AND HOMES OF HONEST AMERICAN FAMILIES. FAREWELL FREE AMERICA!!!! BUT BIMBO BIDEN BUILT A WALL AROUND HIS BEACH HOUSE BASEMENT BUNKER

WITH THE MONEY HUNTER GOT FROM HIS CHINA FRIENDS! (A BIG WALL FOR ME BUT NONE FOR THEE!!!! NEXT THE MASTER OF CEREMONY CORN-HOLE-CORN POP PUT ON A NATIONAL TV SODOM AND GOMORRAH SHOW FOR MR. AND MR, MRS PETE AND CLOSE FRIENDS LIKE "SAMMY" THE BEHIND CLOSE FRIEND OF MRS. PETE.!!! WITH A LINE OF DRAG QUEENS OF JOE AND HUNTER. JOE SHOW YOUR TRUE COLORS!!!! SOUNDS LIKE SODOM AND GOMORRAH ARE MAKING A SECOND COMING. THE BEST ADVICE FOR REAL MEN WORKING THE WHITE NUT HOUSE IS TO INVEST IN STEEL-PLATED UNDERWEAR!

ANOTHER DEMONIC DEMOCRAT PARTY DISASTER! WONDER WHAT CAUSE THE BREAST FORMULA SHORTAGE? THE ANSWER IS THE FACT THAT OUR CLUELESS PRESIDENT MOVED THE WHITE HOUSE TO THE OUTSIDE HOUSE IN ONLY 16 MONTHS! WHEN THE GERIATIC LEFT PARTY GETS FULLER OF SIT THE MORE TOILET PAPER YOU NEED! BRAIN DEAD BIDEN'S SOLUTION IS TO HAVE FARMERS GROW MORE (WHITE CORN) THE COBS ARE MUCH SOFTER NOT LIKE YELLOW JOHN WAYNE CORN WHICH IS ROUGH AND TOUGH AND WON'T TAKE ANY CRAP OFF ANYONE! WHITE CORN COBS ARE LIKE DALE EVANS, SOFT AND PAINLESS!!! ALSO, JOE WANTS PETE TO RAMP UP THE SUPPLY OF PREP H FOR SLEEPY JOE. THE NUMBER 1 PAIN IN THE USA'S REAR END!

"HELP"
SOMEONE PLEASE GO TO NEW YORK AND WAKE UP THE QUEEN OF GLOBAL WARMING! IN THE SOUTH I CAN'T GO OUTSIDE AND MAKE SNOWBALLS! I DON'T NEED TO NOW, I ALREADY HAVE 2

OF MY OWN IN MY HOUSE SINCE I CAN'T AFFORD THE GAS TO HEAT MY HOME !!!!

AOC PLEASE OPEN THAT GIANT RED-LIPPED MOUTH AND BLOW SOME OF THAT GLOBAL WARMING TO THE SOUTH !!! DRILL MORE NATURAL GAS (NOT FROM COWS BEHIND OIL FROM THE GROUND-- NOT THE NATIONAL OIL RESERVE...AND DEFROST MY SNOWBALLS IN MY OWN HOUSE!!!!!!

RESPECTFULLY

THE FROZEN RED GATOR.

THANK YOU JOE

FOR THE SECURE SOUTHERN BORDER!!!

THOUSANDS OF DAILY ILLEGAL ENTRIES.

HUNDREDS OF RAPED 8-12 YEAR OLD GIRLS!

OVER 107,000 DEATHS FROM THE DRUGS MADE BY YOUR #1 FINANCIAL FRIEND PRES CHI PING!!

BUYING THE WORLD'S MOST FILTHY-DIRTY OIL FROM SOUTH AMERICAN COMMUNIST

COUNTRY (VENEZUELA)

YOU KNOW HOW TO MAKE THE AMERICAN PEOPLE HAPPY-WEALTHY AND SECURE!!!!!

I PRAY YOUR BRAIN AWAKENS!!!

CHRISTMAS (LGBTO) 2022

HELP JOE, MY CHILDREN ARE TOTALLY

CONFUSED AFTER YOUR DRAG QUEEN CHRISTMAS PARTY? MY BOYS AND GIRLS DON'T KNOW IF CHRISTMAS SONGS SHOULD BE STOPPED IF THEY SEE DADDY KISSING DAD

"MOMMY» UNDERNEATH THE CHRISTMAS TI

LAST NIGHT!!!!

IS TIME TO START GETTING THE WORLD STRAIGHT BACK TO GOD!

1928 REPEATS ITSELF IN 2022
IN 1928 DEMOCRATIC PRES SAID HE WOULD PUT A CHICKEN IN EVERY POT!!!!
2022 DEMOCRAT GOV. HOKUL SAID SHE COULD RECYCLE YOUR PARENTS PUT THE REMAINS IN A POT AND GROW YOUR OWN
"POT"
THE MARK OF THE BEAST HAS ARRIVED ON THE SCENE-(THE DEMONIC-JACK ASS-BRAIN DEAI CORN POP AND HIS DRAG QUEEN CABINET.
(D) THE MARK OF THE BEAST!!!!!

"DEMS MOTTO JAN.6,2023"
GOD PUT US DEMS HERE TO GET SOMETHING DONE BUT WE ARE SO FAR BEHIND WE WILL NEVER DIE!!!!!
JAN. 6,2023 CEREMONY
"NO PRAYER FOR THE ONLY PERSON KILLED ON JAN 6. IN THE CAPITAL!!!!!! REP.ASHLEY GOPHER!!!
TODAY'S CEREMONY AT THE CAPITAL FOR ME WAS A DISGRACE TO ALL AMERICANS. THE DISASTER THAT HAPPENED WAS THE FAULT OF THE BRAIN DEAD DEMONIC DEMOCRATIC LEADERS OF THE HOUSE, SENATE, AND DC MAYOR!!! IF COL. CUSTER HAD BEEN OFFERED THE HELP OF 1000 ADDITIONAL CALVARY THE BATTLE OF LITTLE BIGHORN WOULD NEVER HAVE HAPPENED!!!!!! WE KNOW THAT THE ONLY DEATH THAT HAPPENED THAT DAY WAS 1 UNARMED REP. A WOMAN, STANDING WITH HER ARMS BY HER SIDE WAS SHOT AND KILLED BY DC CAPITOL POLICEMAN. TO THIS DAY NO ACTION HAS BEEN TAKEN AGAINST THE OFFICER!!!!! THE (DEMONIC (D) PARTY IS A TOTAL DISGRACE BEFORE GOD ALMIGHTY

"TAX THE POOR JOE"
NO NEW TAX ON ANYONE MAKING LESS THAN $400,000 A YEAR!!!! BS!!!!

NOW HE HIRES 87,000 GUN-TOTING IRS AGENTS TO TAX LOW-INCOME TIP EARNERS!!!!
I AM A 100% DISABLED AND DEEMED UNEMPLOYABLE VIET NAM VET. I NOW MAKE 45,000 A YEAR, I HAVE HAD SEVERE PTSD SINCE 1970. I PROMISE YOU IF I GET A LETTER FROM YOUR WEAPONIZED IRS FOR MORE TAX, YOU WILL BE GETTING A SPECIAL DELIVERY GIFT FROM YOUR TRANSPORTATION GENIUS IF UPS DOES NOT GO UNDERGROUND FIRST. YOUR GIFT WILL BE A CIVIL WAR CANNON FOR YOU TO PLAY CORN-HOLE WITH!!!! I KNOW YOU ARE A BIG A-HOLE AND CAN HANDLE THIS. HAVE FUN BIMBO !!! CORN-POP
NO PREP H FOR YOU!!!!!!

ONLY IN AMERICA!!!
CAN AN INDIVIDUAL BE BORN WITH A LOWER-THAN-NORMAL AMOUNT OF GRAY MATTER
BETWEEN THEIR EARS THEY CHEAT THEIR WAY THROUGH LAW SCHOOL. GO 50 YEARS. IN POLITICS UNABLE TO MAKE 1 CORRECT MILITARY DECISION. THEN BE ELECTED BY MILLIONS OF EQUALLY BRAIN-DEFICIENT INDIVIDUALS TO BE THE MOST INCOMPETENT ORALLY AND MENTALLY ILL-EQUIPPED PRESIDENTS IN THE ENTIRE UNIVERSE!!!! WARNING TO ALL 100% MALES WHO INTEND TO VISIT THE (OUT-HOUSE-WHITE HOUSE AND TALK WITH THE MASTER OF DISASTER OF TRANSPORTATION MAYOR SWEETIE!! PETIE!! AKA THE ORIGINAL "CORN HOLE" CHAMPION !!!!!! BE SURE TO WEAR YOUR STEEL-REINFORCED JOCKEY SHORTS TO PREVENT ANY UNEXPECTED REAR-END ATTACK
"AKA" CORN HOLE INCIDENTS!!!!! JOE ALSO CLAIMS TO BE A DEDICATED CATHOLIC! I WAS RAISED IN THIS CHURCH AND WHEN WE MAI THE SIGN OF THE CROSS WE TOUCHED OUR FOREHEAD IN THE NAME OF THE FATHER, THE HEART IN THE NAME OF THE SON, LEFT.

SHOULDER IN THE NAME OF THE HOLY GHOST AND THE RIGHT SHOULDER AMEN.
JOE SAYS IN THE NAME OF CHUCK-NANCY-MAD MAXINE AND ALL MAGA REPS.GO TO HELL!!!!!
"AMEN"
RIP JOE

A MIRACLE CLEANING OF THE CLOSED SOUTHERN BORDER!!!!
TODAY FINALLY THE BRAIN-DEAD LEADER AND HIS EQUALLY EMPTY-HEADED IMMIGRATION CZAR Q-BALL HEADED MAORI KISS! IT WAS REPORTED BOTH
SEEMED TO BE HAVING EXCITED DREAMS WHILE ON THE FLIGHT TO THE OVERRUN BORDER! JOE WAS HAVING DREAMS LIKE SUGAR PLUMS DANCING IN HIS HEAD!!
(NO!!) HE WAS DREAMING OF SMELLING THE HAIR OF ALL THE MULTITUDE OF BEAUTIFUL, YOUNG IMMIGRANT GIRLS' HEADS!!!!
MAYORKISS*** WAS SEEING THE 5 TIMES OVERLOADED STAGING BORDER WAS CLOSED!!!
LOW AND BEHOLD BIDEN'S MILITARY MAID
SERVICE CLEARED THE HUNGRY COLD SLEEPING IN THE STREET MIGRANTS!!!! THERE WAS NOT AN ILLEGAL MIGRANT IN SIGHT!!!!! NOT 1 PERSON LOOKING FOR A FREE PHONE OR FREE PLANE TICKET TO ANYWHERE USA!!!!!
HE SET THE STAGE FOR A BEAUTIFUL PHOTO 10OT FOR THE MEMBERS OF THE SOCIALIST-COMMUNIST USA OF CHINA NO LONGER

NEW TV SHOW!! NOT TUBE-MAN TUBIN ON FAKE NEWS CNN.
DISCOVERY OF JOE BIDEN TOP SECRET PAPERS FOUND IN BIDENS TOP SECRET GARAGE PROTECTED BY HIS CORVETTE!!!! LOCKED!!!!

WELL TRUMP'S VAULT WAS LOCKED AND RELOCKED BY BIDENS COMPROMISED "FBI"

AS I HAVE SAID BEFORE (JOE READ YOUR BIBLE NOT YOUR KORAN)!!! THE BIBLE SAYS WHAT'S DONE IN DARKNESS WILL COME TO THE LIGHT AND BE SHOUTED FROM THE ROOFTOPS!!!!

AS WE SPEAK TRUMP IS STANDING ON THE ROOF OF THE OUT HOUSE WHITE HOUSE SHOUTING GO JOE GO!! AROUND THE BOWL AND DOWN THE HOLE GO JOE GO!!!! JOE YOU ARE FREE TO CALL ME ANYTIME @200-690-U812—-DRAG QUEEN!!!!!

JAN 18,2023
SHAME ON YOU BIMBO BIDEN. YOUR LYING PRESS SECRETARY STATED THAT YOU WERE VERY CONCERNED ABOUT THE SAFETY OF ALL AMERICAN CITIZENS. (BULL MANURE!!!!!)

JAN. 17 2023 6 PEOPLE WERE MURDERED BY POSSIBLE MEXICAN CARTEL MEMBERS. 1 GRANDMOTHER, 1 16 YR.OLD MOTHER, AND HER

10 MONTH OLD CHILD. ALL WERE SHOT IN THE BACK OF THE HEAD AND 4 OTHER FAMILY MEMBERS WERE KILLED BY POSSIBLE MEXICAN CARTEL MEMBERS YOU WELCOMED WITH OPEN ARMS THROUGH YOUR (FULLY OPEN) CLOSED BORDER!!!

HAVE FUN AND ENJOY THE "TRUTH" ALSO I FULLY APPROVE OF REPARATION FOR ALL AMERICANS WHO HAVE THE USE OF THEIR ARMS, LEGS, HANDS, AND MOUTH! IF YOU QUALIFY YOU NEED TO GET OFF YOUR DO-NOTHING REAR END AND GET A (JOB) NOT SMASH AND GRAB.

I AM SICK OF THE EXCUSE I NEED SOMETHING TO EAT!!!! I'M WAITING TO SEE SOMEONE EAT A FUR COAT, ROLEX WATCH OR DIAMOND RING. YOU ARE PUTTING

COMPANIES OUT OF BUSINESS AND PUTTING RESIDENTS OF THE COMMUNITY OUT OF A "JOB". A JOB IS A REPARATION!
A PAYCHECK EVERY WEEK IS A JUST REWARD! NO HURT-HARM-OR DANGER!!!
JOB-AKA-REPARATION!!!!!! GET UP & SHUT UP!!!!!!

JAN 24,2023
INADVERTENTLY MY BIG RED GATOR REAR END!!
OVER 1850 BOXES OF CLASSIFIED BOXES OF GOVERNMENT DOCUMENTS !!!! C=MON MAN!!
BILL CLINTON HAD AN INADVERTENTLY HEAD-TO-HEAD UNION UNDER HIS DESK IN THE [OVAL] OFFICE WITH MONICA IN A BLUE DRESS WITH A STRANGE STAIN ON THE FRONT OF THE DRESS!!!!! INADVERTENTLY JEFF "TUBE-MAN TUBIN" CHOKED HIS CHICKEN BEHIND HIS DESK ON NATIONAL TV!!!!! I WONDER IF JEFF IS CLOSE FRIENDS WITH IR. AND MRS.MR. PETE OR SAMMY THE NUCLEAR WASTE MAN!!!! DON'T FORGET
DON LAMON"

JOE'S CLAIMED ACCOMPLISHMENTS SINCE 2020!
BEST ECONOMY IN 50 YEARS. FALSE HIGHEST INFLATION =TRUE HIGHEST FUEL COST-TRUE HIGHEST FOOD COST-TRUE HIGHEST USED CAR PRICES-TRUE
HIGHEST STORE CLOSINGS DUE TO THEFT-TRUE
HIGHEST ILLEGAL MIGRANTS-TRUE
HIGHEST SCHOOL KIDS FAILURE RATE-TRUE
HIGHEST DEATH RATES FROM CHINESE DRUGS-TRUE
PRESIDENT WITH BRUISED KNEES FROM FALLING CLIMBING UP AIR FORCE ONE STEPS VP WITH MOST WORD SALADS IN HISTORY TRUE HIGHEST SELLING COCAINE PIPE PAINTINGS-TRUE

HIGHEST-PRICED RUSSIAN ESCORTS- TRUE WORLD
WORST TOILET PAPER WITH JOE'S FACE ON EACH SHEET!
ITS LIKE JOHN WAYNE ROUGH AND TOUGH AND DON'T
TAKE NO CRAP OFF NOBODY. TOUGHER THAN BAD CORN
POP!!
TRUTH!! WITHOUT THE CONSTANT DAILY LIES AND
BLUNDERS FROM JOE BOOK WOULD BE POSSIBLE!!!!
OWE IT ALL TO YOU [BIG GUY] JOE!!!!!

HAIL TO THE PASSING OF THE GUARD
/ WAS ALWAYS TAUGHT THAT SATAN WAS THE FATHER
OF ALL LIES!! WELCOME THE NEW FATHER SLEEPY JOE
BIDEN. / WILL UNITE THE COUNTRY— LIE. / WILL NOT PAY
ILLEGAL INDIVIDUALS WHO COME TO THIS COUNTRY
TO KILL, RAPE, STEAL AND DISRESPECT THE LAWS OF
THIS COUNTRY---LIE! I WILL PROTECT THE PEOPLE AND
LAWS OF THIS COUNTRY - LIE. OPEN BORDERS DO NOT
PROTECT THE CITIZENS OF THE USA. TAX PAYER $450.000
WALL AROUND BIDEN BEACH HOUSE.
WONDERFUL?
/ WILL LEAVE NO AMERICAN BEHIND!!LIE—
HUNDREDS LEFT-BILLIONS OF $'S LEFT BEHIND! LIE!
VP STARTED A FUND TO PAY BAIL FOR CRIMINALS TO
BURN CITIES, AND FEDERAL BUILDINGS ATTACK POLICE,
AND BLIND SOME. FANTASTIC!!!!
ICE WORLD LEADER OF OIL AND GAS-NOW SAR OF APAC
TO PRODUCE MORE FOR US.

JOE BIDEN NOW CROWNED THE FORERUNNER OF THE
ANTICHRIST!!!! IN THE BIBLE YOU MUST HAVE THE MARK
OF THE BEAST TO BUY!! WITH ANTICHRIST BIDEN YOU
MUST SHOW
ID TO GO TO A RESTAURANT- GYM- AND SOCIAL
GATHERINGS. JOE ID IS A MANDATORY PUNCTURE THAT

MAY OR MAY NOT PROTECT YOU OR OTHERS. MARK OF THE BIDEN BEAST!!!
BIDEN BATTLE CRY [RULES FOR YOU - NOT FOR ME!!! HAIL THE NEW FATHER OF ALL LIES AND THE ANTI-CHRIST FORERUNNER. JOE BIMBO BIBEN!!!
PAY YOUR FAIR SHARE JOE AND HUNTER!!!!!

THE DECEIVING CONVERSATIONS OF BIDEN AND NANCY {RULES FOR YOU BUT NOT FOR ME!!!!! POLICIES UNDER COVER!
SHOULD A WISE MAN UTTER VAIN
KNOWLEDGE AND FILL HIS BELLY WITH THE EAST WIND? SHALL HE REASON WITH UNPROFITABLE TALK? OR WITH SPEECHES WHEREWITH HE CAN DO NO GOOD?
YEA THOUGH CASTETH OUT FEAR AND RESTRAINT PRAYER BEFORE GOD.
FOR THY MOUTH UTTERETH THINE INIQUITY AND THOU CHOOSEST THINE THE TONGUE OF THE CRAFTY, THINE OWN LIPS TESTIFY AGAINST THEE. TELL THE TRUTH DEMOCRATS !!!!!!

PRIOR PROPER PLANNING PREVENTS PISS-POOR PERFORMANCE! 1111
EXAMPLE TRUMP'S NON-COMBAT TROOPS LOST AFGHAN WITHDRAWAL!!!
NUMBER 2 SCHOOL OF BIDEN'S TYPICAL IGNORANT 7-P'S NO PROPER PRIOR PLANNING GREATLY PROVIDES HORRIBLE COMBAT TROOP DEATH AND DESTRUCTION AND PISS POOR PERFORMANCE!!!
THE WORST IN MILITARY HISTORY!!!!! NO BRAIN-NO PAIN!!!!

BRAIN-DEAD BIMBO BIDEN WANTS TO PAY ILLEGAL CRIMINAL IMMIGRANTS WHO MAY HAVE LOST THEIR UNDOCUMENTED CHILDREN AFTER BEING LOCKED

UP IN CAGES BUILT BY THE OBAMA ADMINISTRATION! PAY $450,000 EACH. HOW MANY AMERICAN CHILDREN HAVE BEEN KIDNAPPED BY ILLEGAL IMMIGRANTS NEVER TO BE FOUND? HOW MANY AMERICAN PARENTS HAVE BEEN PAID—(0)-THE LAW IN THE USA YOU ARE NOT TO PUT CHILDREN IN JAIL WITH ILLEGAL ADULT PARENTS! WHAT ABOUT ALL THE AMERICANS KILLED BY ILLEGALS, DRUNK DRIVERS AND RAPIST! DID THEY GET PAID? THE RADICAL LEFT DEMONIC DEMOCRATS ARE LEADING THE MOST POWERFUL NATION INTO THE PATH OF SELF-DESTRUCTION!! WE MUST STOP THE WOKE ANTI-AMERICAN CULTURE! GOD ABOVE IS WATCHING IN DISGRACE BIDEN DESTROYING HIS GREATEST CREATION!! GOD BLESS AMERICA, THE LAND OF THE SO FAR SOCIALISM, MARXIST COMMUNISM LAND OF THE FREE!!!!!! I'M WATCHING TRUE NEWS ON TV AND AM WITNESSING THE MOST INTELLIGENT CONVERSATION EVER EMITTED BY THE BRAIN DEAD PRESIDENT JOE BIDEN WHILE ON THE NATIONAL STAGE WITH THE QUEEN OF ENGLAND'S SON, JOE SPOKE THE MOST INTELLIGENT WORDS HE EVER SPOKE. HE SPOKE STRAIGHT FROM HIS TOOTHLESS WONDER GREAT LIPS OF FIRE BEHIND------BERRRAPH !!!!!!! ALL THEY COULD DO IS LOOK AT EACH OTHER AND GIVE THEIR BEST EDITION OF THE FAMOUS KAMALA HORSE LAUGH!!!!!
THIS IS THE LARGEST EMISSION OF GREEN NEW GAS KNOWN TO MAN !!!!!
E BE LIKE LITTLE BOY BLUE AND BLOW YOUR HORN ALL OVER THE WHITE USE!!!!!

THE ANTICHRIST HAS ARRIVED AND IS HARD AT WORK!!! IF YOU DO NOT HAVE THE "MARK OF THE BEAST COVID (D) YOU CAN NOT EAT INDOORS, FLY ON A PLANE OR GO TO THE MOVIES OR HOLD A JOB TO SUPPORT YOUR FAMILY: THE ANTICHRIST JOE BIMBO BIDEN AND HIS

ARMY THE SOCIALIST DEMONIC DEMOCRAT PARTY SAID ONCE ILLEGAL IMMIGRANTS ARE IN THE USA THAT ICE WILL NOT BE ABLE TO LOCATE THEM FOR DEPORTATION: "BULL'S-IT" BILLIONAIRES HAVE MICROCHIPS INJECTED INTO THEIR CHILDREN AND PETS IN CASE A CROOK WANTS RANSOM FOR THEIR RETURN!!! INSERT A CHIP INCLUDING THE COVID-19 VACCINE IN ALL ILLEGAL IMMIGRANTS OVER 10YRS, OLD. THIS WOULD ALSO BE A GREAT POLICY FOR ALL RADICAL LEFT DAS WHEN LETTING DANGEROUS CRIMINALS OUT EARLY. YOU CAN RUN BUT YOU CANNOT HIDE!!!!
THE BIBLE SAYS WHAT'S DONE IN DARKNESS WILL CON TO THE LIGHT AND BE SHOUTED FROM THE ROOF TO VO SHOT-NO JOB PER ANTICHRIST JOE BIDEN.
AMEN AND AMEN

ALL RADICAL LEFT DEMONIC
DEMOCRAT MEN ARE
ENDOWLED WITH "DICKIE DOS" THAT MEANS THEIR BELLIES STICK OUT FARTHER THAN THEIR "DICKIES DO" !!!!

THE DECEIVING CONVERSATIONS OF BIDEN AND NANCY RULES FOR YOU BUT NOT FOR ME!!!! POLICIES UNDER COVER!
SHOULD A WISE MAN UTTER VAIN
KNOWLEDGE AND FILL HIS BELLY WITH THE EAST WIND? SHALL HE REASON WITH UNPROFITABLE TALK? OR WITH SPEECHES WHEREWITH HE CAN DO NO GOOD?
YEA THOUGH CASTETH OUT FEAR AND RESTRAINT PRAYER BEFORE GOD.
FOR THY MOUTH UTTERETH THINE INIQUITY AND THOU CHOOSEST THINE THE TONGUE OF THE CRAFTY. THINE OWN LIPS TESTIFY AGAINST THEE. THE TRUTH DEMOCRATS !!!!!

FROM A 100% DISABLED VIETNAM VETERAN!!!!
[JOE BIDEN JUSTICE]
TOP BIDEN MILITARY LEADERS
LIE TO PROTECT LYING PRESIDENT BIDEN!!!
WHEN A JUNIOR MILITARY
OFFICER TELLS THE TRUTH
"HOLY SH-T" LOCK HIM UP-LOCK HIM UP.
LAWS ARE FOR THEE NOT FOR ME.

BYE ANTICHRIST JOE, CRAZY NANCY, AND ALL RADICAL
LEFT DEMOCRATS. I WILL MISS YOU ALL LIKE THE
REMOVAL OF INFECTED BOIL ON TOP OF A HEMORRHOID!!!
NO MORE PAIN THE BEHIND OR IN THE WALLET!!!!!!
RELIEF AT LAST "HELLO
DONALD TRUMP"

PAYBACK PENALTIES FOR BIMBO BIDENS MANDATORY
VACCINATIONS:
ANYONE WHO CAN PROVE A NEGATIVE REACTION FROM
FORCED VACCINATION WILL BE
PAID $100,000 FROM THE BIDEN ADMIN. ANYWHO DIED
AS A RESULT OF THE SHOT OF THEIR FAMILY WILL BE
PAID ONE MILLION FROM THE BIDEN FAMILY ACCOUNT.
PAY YOUR FAIR SHARE JOE!!!!!

TODAY I HEARD THAT OUR EQUALLY INEPT UNCONSCIOUS
VICE PRESIDENT IS GETTING HER WISH TO GO TO
EUROPE TO PURSUE THE OUT-OF-HAN PROBLEM WITH
EUROPE'S BORDER DISASTER----ILLEGAL IMMIGRANTS!
SHE REFUSED TO ADDRESS THE PROBLEM IN THE USA
DUE TO IGNORANCE OF THE SITUATION ON HER PART
AND THE LACK OF ACTION FROM HER (BOSS). SOUND
ASLEEP JOE BIDEN!!! MEANWHILE BACK IN THE SINKING
USA BIMBO'S NOW THINKING ABOUT SHUTTING DOWN
ANOTHER MUCH-NEEDED OIL SUPPLY LINE!!!! ONLY A

MARXIST SOCIALIST BRAIN-DEAD INDIVIDUAL COULD CONTRIVE!!!! THIS IS EXACTLY WHY THE KEEPERS OF OUT OF HIS MIND BID WAS KEPT AWAY FROM THE PUBLIC DURING THE ELECTION PROCESS.

SOUNDING THE RACE WHISTLE BEFORE THE ELECTION WAS THE MOST RA EXTREMIST BIMBO BIDEN!!!! HE NEEDED THE MINORITY VOTE AND WHO WOULD SELECT AN AFRICAN AMERICAN WOMAN FOR VP.!!IT WORKED / ROBERT BYRD ROLLED OVER IN HIS RACIST GRAVE!!!! C'MON MAN!!!!

AS AN AFTERTHOUGHT!!! I WAS JUST WONDERING IF THE BORDER CZI TO EUROPE ON HER "AOC" DESIGNED NEW GREEN GAS POWERED HORSE LAUGHING ALL THE WAY---CAMELA!!!!!

WHEN YOU ARE A 17-YEAR-OLD WHITE MALE AND YOUR FATHER'S HOME HOMETOWN IS BURNED TO THE GROUND BY HATE GROUPS AND BLM RIOTERS AND YOU COME TO TOWN TO HELP PROTECT PRIVATE PROPERTY, DO MINOR FIRST AID, AND HELP PUT OUT FIRES. THEN YOU GET IN DEADLY TROUBLE WITH RIOTERS AND IN SELF-DEFENSE KILL 2 PEOPLE AND WOUND 1. THEN THE PRESIDENT GOES ON NATL. TV AND CALLS YOU A WHITE SUPREMACIST. GUILTY-GUILTY. THIS FOR THE TIME BEING IS THE LAND WHERE YOU ARE INNOCENT UNTIL PROVEN GUILTY BY A GROUP OF YOUR PEERS. WHAT SAY YOU JOE !! DID YOU TURN THE COUNTRY OVER TO YOUR FRIEND (PUTIN)? DON'T FORGET XI! THIS IS STILL FOR THE TIME BEING THE "USA '' NOT THE USSR. C'MON MAN !!!!!

THE BIBEN ADMIN IS PRETENDING TO BE THE CREW OF THE STARSHIP ENTERPRISE! BIDEN: CAPTAIN KIRK POTHOLE PETE: SPOCK KAMALA HARRIS COMM; SPEC: LT. UHURA

ADAM SCHIFF: GIANT FINGER-INTERPLANETARY PROCTOLOGIST!

THEIR MISSION WAS TO TRAVEL TO THE PLANET UR-ANUS AND WIPE OUT ALL CLING-ONS AND APPLY A GOOD COAT OF PREP-H TO ALL ALIENS!!!

WHY JOE CANNOT READ!!!

WHEN JOEY WAS A YOUNG TEENAGER AND WAS UPSTAIRS IN HIS BEDROOM HIS DAD WAS WALKING UP THE STAIRS AND HE HEARD A STRANGE CHANT COMING FROM JOEY BOYS ROOM.

WHEN DAD GOT TO THE DOOR HE HEARD JOE SINGING DON'T GIVE A DAMN IF I DO DIE-DO DIE. I JUST WANT TO SEE THE JUICE FLY-JUICE FLY!!! DAD TOLD HIS SON. JOEY BOY IF YOU DON'T STOP

THAT YOU WILL GO BLIND. THIS IS THE REASON JOE CANNOT READ TODAY! EITHER JOE IS NOT WEARING GLASSES OR HIS DADS WARNING IS COMING TO THE LIGHT!!!

PRESIDENT TRUMP, I HOPE TO SEE YOU AT MARA-LAGO THIS SUMMER, THE MAGA RED GATOR-MAN!!!!! GOD BLESS YOU AND YOUR FAMILY!!!!!!

Printed in the United States
by Baker & Taylor Publisher Services